MOA'S ARK

MOA'S ARK
The Voyage of New Zealand

David Bellamy and
Brian Springett
with Peter Hayden

Principal photographer
Peter Johnson

VIKING

VIKING

Penguin Books (NZ) Ltd, 182–190 Wairau Road, Auckland 10, New Zealand
Penguin Books Ltd, 27 Wrights Lane, London W8 5TZ, England
Viking Penguin Inc, 40 West 23rd Street, New York, New York 10010, USA
Penguin Books Australia Ltd, 487 Maroondah Highway, Ringwood, Australia 3134
Penguin Books Canada Ltd, 2801 John Street, Markham, Ontario, Canada L3R 1B4

Penguin Books Ltd, Registered Offices: Harmondsworth, Middlesex, England

First published in 1990
10 9 8 7 6 5 4 3 2 1

Editorial services by Michael Gifkins and Associates
Design and production by Richard King
Typeset by Typocrafters Ltd, Auckland
Printed in Hong Kong

ISBN 0 670 83098 4

Half-title page: Pirita, a native mistletoe, *Peraxilla colensoi*,
a once-common parasite on beech, now endangered by possums.

Title page: Moonrise over the Poor Knights.
WADE DOAK

CONTENTS

Time-line of Windows   8
Location of Windows   9
Acknowledgements   11
Prologue   13

Part One: Voyage into the Deep Past

(1) *Rotorua Boils*   19
     The Archean period, 3.6 eons to 570 million years ago.
     The age of the bacteria and their kin.

(2) *Milford Sound*   27
     The Cambrian period, 570 to 500 million years ago.
     Life abundant but only in the sea.

(3) *Poor Knights*   32
     The Ordovician period, 500 to 430 million years ago.
     The first coral reefs abound with shells and the first fish.

(4) *Tongariro Records*   36
     The Silurian period, 430 to 400 million years ago.
     Life begins to move onto the land.

(5) *Rangitoto Brinkmanship*   41
     The Devonian period, 400 to 350 million yeas ago.
     The age of the ferns.

(6) *Taranaki Futures*   47
     The Carboniferous period, 350 to 300 million years ago.
     The age of swamps in which coal and other fossil fuels were formed;
     the age of giant amphibians and insects.

(7) *Takitimu Leaves*   52
     The Permian period, 300 to 235 million years ago.
     The age of ferns with seeds and reptiles with eggs.

(8) *Wellington Worms*   55
     The Early to Middle Triassic period, 235 to 208 million years ago.
     The age of the dinosaur and the food plants.

(9) *Waipoua Giants*   59
     The Late Triassic, 208 to 192 million years ago.
     The age of the podocarps.

(10) *Stephens Island*   67
     The Jurassic period, 192 to 135 years ago.
     The dinosaurs give rise to the birds in landscapes dominated by
     cone-bearing plants.

(11) *Whirinaki Podocarps*   71
     The Early Cretaceous period, 135 to 95 million years ago.
     The demise of the dinosaurs and the rise of the flower-bearing plants
     and the mammals. Moa's Ark casts off.

(12) *Te Anau Beech*   76
The Late Cretaceous period, 95 to 65 million years ago.
The end of the dinosaurs and many groups of plants during 'The Great
Extinction'.

Part Two: The Voyage of the Ark

(13) *Bats on Little Barrier*   85
The Paleocene period, 65 to 53 million years ago.
The world is dominated by warm-blooded mammals over most of the
earth, birds in the sanctuary of Moa's Ark.

(14) *Riccarton Bush*   91
The Eocene period, 53 to 37 million years ago.
The earth begins to cool, heading for an age of ice. Penguins take over
the seas and the forest of Moa's Ark.

(15) *Taiaroa Royal Nursery*   97
The Oligocene period, 37 to 24 million years ago.
Antarctica is dying of cold, white death, while new patterns of life are
developing in the southern seas. The seas are dominated by the warm-
blooded whales and dolphins, minds in the waters of the poorly named
planet Earth. .

(16) *Punakaiki Pancakes*   103
The Miocene period, 24 to 5 million years ago.
The main groups of mammals have emerged, including our direct
ancestors, the primates. Moa's Ark sails towards warm waters. Palms
and other tropical plants with some birds are aboard, but snakes and
mammals miss the boat.

(17) *A Day on Bald Mountain*   109
The Pliocene period, 5 to 2 million years ago.
Radiation of the mammals in most land masses except Moa's Ark.
Our earliest definite ancestor makes an appearance.

(18) *The Sky-Piercer*   116
The Pleistocene period, 2 million years to not all that long ago.
The ice ages begin to shape life upon this modern earth as flowering
plants and people spread out in the wake of its destructive creation.

(19) *Franz Josef*   121
The cycle of soil genesis and degradation.

(20) *Pureora and the Big Sneeze*   126
An autumn day in the Holocene period, AD 186.
People are exploiting all the productive lands of the world except those
of Moa's Ark.

Part Three: Raiders of the Last Ark

(21) *Shag Bay Barbecue*   135
AD 900, or thereabouts. People have arrived on deck and Moa's Ark
will never be the same again — the environmental revolution reaches
New Zealand at last.

(22) *Oparara R.I.P.*   140
Five hundred years of destruction when the hunters, fishers and fire-
lighters take their toll.

(23) *The Aupouri Tombolo*   146
The demise of the moa and the moa hunters. The former become extinct,
the latter reach back to find the roots and seeds of their past.

(24) *The Snares*   152
A window onto paradise at risk of being destroyed forever.
The Snares are what it was like before humans set foot in New Zealand.

(25) *Captain Cook*   158
The Europeans arrive and the pace of destructive change moves into
top gear.

(26) *The Bridge to Nowhere*   161
Agriculture in all its changing forms, a bridge to nowhere for some,
a bridgehead into Moa's Ark for too many.

(27) *Raiders of the Last Ark*   167
A biological catastrophe as the story of the Raiders unfolds and an
alphabet of distaster is revealed.

(28) *Kaingaroa Forest*   180
The affluent 1920s, when the great plantations were laid out and
a bountiful future seemed secure.

(29) *Eastwoodhill Arboretum*   185
The ecological disaster area of the east of New Zealand from Gisborne
to Canterbury.

Part Four: Refloating the Ark

(30) *Conservation Kiwi-wise*   195
A window of hope, both individual and institutional, as a conservation
ethic grows.

(31) *To the Lifeboats!*   205
The immediate task of abandoning Moa's Ark and preserving some
of the original passengers.

(32) *Tiritiri Matangi*   210
An open island sanctuary close to Auckland.

(33) *Mahoenui and Mapara*   216
The brave new world of the Department of Conservation.

(34) *Graeme Platt's Place*   219
A green window into the future for all the occupants of Moa's Ark.

Epilogue   223
Index   227

TIME-LINE OF WINDOWS

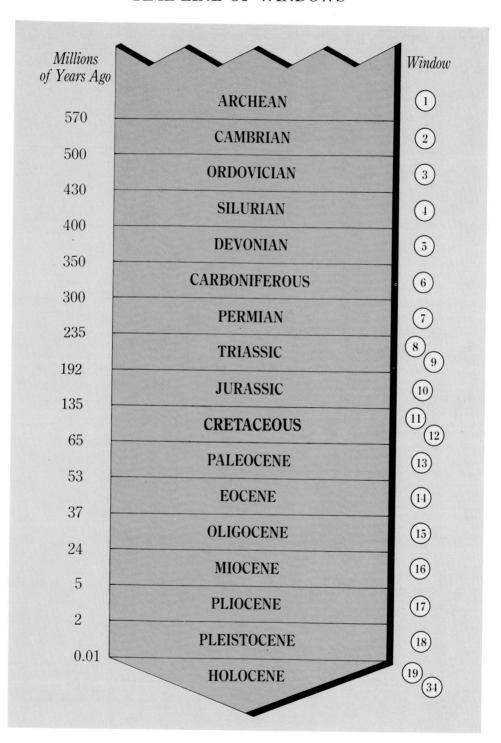

Millions of Years Ago		Window
	ARCHEAN	①
570	CAMBRIAN	②
500	ORDOVICIAN	③
430	SILURIAN	④
400	DEVONIAN	⑤
350	CARBONIFEROUS	⑥
300	PERMIAN	⑦
235	TRIASSIC	⑧ ⑨
192	JURASSIC	⑩
135	CRETACEOUS	⑪ ⑫
65	PALEOCENE	⑬
53	EOCENE	⑭
37	OLIGOCENE	⑮
24	MIOCENE	⑯
5	PLIOCENE	⑰
2	PLEISTOCENE	⑱
0.01	HOLOCENE	⑲ ㉞

LOCATION OF WINDOWS

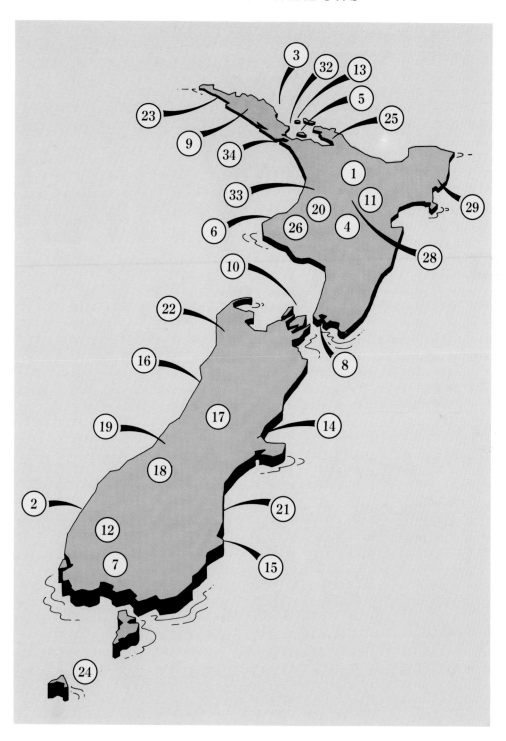

NEW ZEALAND
NATURAL HERITAGE
FOUNDATION

Massey University
Palmerston North

ACKNOWLEDGEMENTS

The Crew of the Good Ship Moa's Ark

Captain	Peter Hayden
Purser	Glenda Norris
First Mate	Michael Lemmon
Bosun	Craig McKersey
Telecommunications Officer	Mervyn Aitchison
Quartermaster	Peter Short
Ship's Botanist	Peter Johnson
Ancient Mariner	David Bellamy
Deckhand	Ian McGee
Ship's Surgeon	Department of Conservation
Engineers	Peter Simkins and Cherie O'Shea

Moa's Ark

Port Authority

Harbour Master	Michael Stedman
Pilot	Brian Springett
Lighthouse Keeper	Delyse Springett

Patrons

New Zealand Natural Heritage Foundation
Television New Zealand
New Zealand Tourist and Publicity Department
Massey University and all the sponsors of the Natural Heritage Foundation

Our grateful thanks are due to:

Barney Brewster for the naming of Moa's Ark
The tangata whenua of Aotearoa
Department of Conservation
Department of Scientific and Industrial Research
Royal Forest and Bird Protection Society
Native Forests Restoration Trust
The Maruia Society
The flora, fauna, geology and soils of New Zealand
All the Kiwis of New Zealand, who care, and who helped us all the way.

The making of the television series carried us the length and breadth of New Zealand. En route we took in the sights and sounds, recording them on film and tape. We also made many new friends, renewed old acquaintances, and, on the way, I had the problem and the pleasure of writing this book; no easy task when you are on the move, and I make no apologies for the blatant plagiarism of conversations, interviews and the contents of the small library I carried with me.

The actual format of the book was the most difficult part of the whole business, but, like Topsy, it just grew and evolved along the way. Each place we visited, each location on the film schedule, became a window through which we could step back into the past, learn from the present and plan for the future. We were on a journey, like Moa's Ark itself, through space and time, weaving a pattern of living heritage. New Zealand is a truly amazing place, a living museum, through the windows of which we were privileged to gaze.

So it was the thirty-four chapters came into being.

David J. Bellamy
New Zealand Natural Heritage Foundation
Massey University
Palmerston North

PROLOGUE

Dear David,

*Here is a stamp for your collection,
it is a picture of Tane Mahuta, the largest
kauri tree in New Zealand.*
    I hope you like it.

Uncle Nem

I am afraid I didn't keep the postcard, but I did keep the stamp, which took pride of place in my collection, introduced me to Aotearoa and perhaps stirred the botanical interests latent in me.

Uncle Nem (who also bought me my first pedal car, with lights that went on and off) worked in the office of the New Zealand High Commission in London, and he told me many stories about that far-off land.

In those days, New Zealanders were often in the headlines, thanks to the part they played in the Second World War; and New Zealand products formed an important part of our meagre wartime rations. Anchor butter, succulent lamb and juicy apples — I can taste them now.

I can also remember the large wooden boxes from which our weekly two-ounce ration of butter was plucked and patted out; and my dad using the boxes for storing all sorts of things in the garden shed, even chopping them for kindling the coal fires that warmed us through those bitter winters. Only much later did I learn that they were made of a very special sort of wood called kahikatea, which, being free from any resin or odour, was ideal to contain the precious cargo. Oh, happy pre-cholesterol days!

For many years New Zealand was, to me, a land of cows, sheep and apple trees. The thought never entered my head — nor, as far as I can recollect, our geography books — that they were not natural denizens of the countryside. The ravages of rabbits in Australia were the butt of many jokes on radio, but as far as I was concerned, cows and sheep were as natural a part of the New Zealand scene as volcanoes, hot springs and geysers.

As my education progressed, my knowledge of New Zealand was not improved. It seemed only natural that their young men and women should cross the world to die for their 'King and Country', or that some of Britain's population should emigrate to open up new land, new business and to forge new hopes for a commonwealth of nations.

In chronological order, my next contact with New Zealand was when, as a botany undergraduate, I had to study the structure of *Tmesipteris*: a plant the textbooks informed me grew on the trunks of tree ferns and was very like the first plants to develop leaves, almost 350 million years ago. We had only one leaf at college, and that was well and truly pickled, so I toured the botanic gardens, only to find that there were no specimens of this unique plant growing in captivity. My search led me to the library of the British Museum of Natural History in Kensington. There I was introduced to the works of Leonard Cockayne on the flora of New Zealand and to the fact that in 1839 some strange bones arrived in London, bones that were later identified as belonging to a great bird named the moa.

As I read more and more, the Land of the Long White Cloud took on a new fascination for me: a land of botanical treasures, of ferns and their close relatives, some of which had first stood upright on earth more than 350 million years ago; of trees, mighty enough to have sheltered dinosaurs; and of flower-bearing plants that evolved unmolested by the teeth of herbivorous mammals. A land of wonder and of world records, like the largest . . . but no, you must wait, the goodies are to come as the story unfolds.

It's funny how you bump into Kiwis all over the world, and it's not just a recent phenomenon. I attended lectures by Professor Val Chapman, famed for his work on the ecology of mangroves and Pacific islands. My wife was a student of Professor John Morton, who inspired thousands of students to follow littoraly (that means between the tides) in his beach-combing footsteps. John is a scientist, artist and communicator of the highest order, but, above and around all, a Christian. We were sorry to see him leave London University and move back to his native Auckland as Professor of Zoology. Les Turnbull made the transition the other way and came to lecture at Bedford College, London University, where I did my PhD. He stayed on to become Registrar and further inspired me with tales of his homeland; tales of valleys and mountains, of forests, grasslands and bogs whose natural history was still *Terra incognita*.

I couldn't wait to get there and see it for myself, but I had to remain impatient for a long time. This impatience was fanned by the fact that I found myself teaching courses on biogeography, the discipline that concerns itself with the reason why certain plants and animals are only found in certain parts of the world; plant ecology, the science of why and how certain plants grow where they do; and phytosociology, the study of the communities of plants. It was my turn to tantalise my students with snippets of information about New Zealand, and two of them, Maurice Kerman and Keith Thompson, made the transworld flit before me to become naturalised Kiwi lecturers. Again I had to wait, consoling myself with more and more facts about a land whose area was 268,676 square kilometres, made up of more than 700 islands, two large and some very small, and which was home to some of the world's rarest and most endangered plants and animals.

At last I met the Kiwi who helped make almost thirty years of my dreams come true. Randal Beatty started his media career with TVNZ and was a director with Thames Television in London when we started working on the scripts of *Botanic Man (A Journey Through Evolution)*. So it was only natural that New Zealand should play a key role in the development of the story, indeed, the starring role it has in the evolution of our living world.

Travel not only broadens the mind, but also shatters many misconceptions gained from afar. The written word can and does mislead: eyeball contact with people and places focuses images and clarifies concepts.

New Zealand provided us with all the images and all the live action we needed for those key parts of *Botanic Man*, but it also provided me with some short, sharp shocks.

I had always thought that in such an environmentally and economically rich country with a relatively tiny population, when it came to looking after so many unique and important plants and animals there should be no problems. New Zealand, the last large piece of real estate to be discovered by humankind, was surely an ark, safe enough to guard its precious cargo of the products of creative evolution on their voyage into the future. How wrong or how right could I be?

Once again, I was to meet someone who would push my New Zealand adventures on their way. Or, to tell the truth, we met again. Professor Brian Springett was a PhD student at Durham University when I arrived there as a junior lecturer, and we renewed our contact when I stayed at Brian's home during the ANZAAS Conference at Massey University, New Zealand, in January 1987.

Over the Springetts' kitchen table, Brian and Delyse and I had some of those talks that change the courses of lives. We pooled ideas that led to the formation of the New Zealand Natural Heritage Foundation, which would develop a major programme including a comprehensive film on New Zealand's natural heritage, with accompanying books, school resources and tourism trails. They were seminal discussions that we held there, night after night, and that kitchen table has a lot to answer for!

So has Dr Neil Waters, Vice-Chancellor of Massey University, who gave us not only the permission but the direction to go ahead. By the time Brian had talked to another visionary, Michael Stedman, head of TVNZ's Natural History Department, the major film series was on, and my learning curve went into orbit.

So it was that *Moa's Ark* landed firmly on the drawing board.

PART ONE

Voyage into the Deep Past

◀ Fossil forest at Curio Bay, Southland, exposed at low tide.

Rotorua Boils

Fossil fuel pulsed faster through burnished copper tubes; the pitch of four in line increased; and in response, the Tiger Moth climbed up and over in a perfect loop-the-loop. A rim of rolling green, studded with neat farmsteads, grazing sheep and lollipop trees each with shadows cast by the setting sun, slipped down and out of view. One hundred and eighty degrees of blue, blue, blue, clouded with golden-grey-white slid by, then a moment of velvet green again. Soon, an ordered patchwork of roads appeared, appliquéd with hotels, motels, BYO inlets, fastfood outlets, shops and homes, complete with telltale wisps of vapour. Fast forward, in barrel-roll replay, strained both mind and machine into momentary oblivion.

I was given this grandstand view from a tiny aircraft over Rotorua, topped off with aerobatics: the ultimate experience in the steam-driven, four-ringed circus of tourism which keeps Rotorua as New Zealand's number one tourist hotspot.

The four rings are the ancient calderas of Taupo, Maroa, Okataina and Rotorua. Each is the result of collapse following massive volcanic activity and each is complete with whip-crack faults reaching down to tap the heat of the molten magma not so deep in the earth's crust.

Every year tourists come to see the 'Greatest Show of Geothermal Activity on Earth', with, top of the bill, Whakarewarewa. The show comes complete with a Maori arts and crafts centre, hot springs, gas vents, mud volcanoes, bubbling mud pools advertised as ideal to soothe the tourist's troubled brow — and, of course, the geysers. Not only does volcanic activity throw up some of earth's most spectacular rock-twisting phenomena, it also generates some fascinating and tongue-twisting words: words you must master if you are going to get the most out of your visit to these geothermal fields. Roll up, roll up! Here are a couple of starters: ignimbrite and sinter — rock stars in their own right. Top of the volcanic pops, ignimbrites are a product of the molten magma, a form of pumice ranging from the finest of the fine to quite large lumps, which are explosively ejected from the earth prior to caldera formation.

The whole world heard about the eruption of Mount St Helens in the USA. It shot out a mere three cubic kilometres of volcanic material with devastating effects in May 1980. Compare that with the eruption which led to the collapse of the earth's crust and the formation of the caldera of Rotorua. Then, 200 cubic kilometres of Mamaku ignimbrites were blasted out to cover 400 square kilometres of the local landscape. Think with awe about that figure, for it represents enough new rock to cover an area the extent of London with a mound of ash two kilometres high — and be thankful that this mammoth event took place 140,000 years ago! With all that magma gone, plastered over the local landscapes, it is little wonder that the surface of the land collapsed to form a fifteen-kilometre-wide depression: the all-action caldera of Rotorua, complete with lots of sinter.

Sinter is a much more gentle sort of rock, laid down in the quietest of ways by the precipitation of minerals dissolved in hot water. Sinter is made of silica, and so is glass. Silica is one of the most common chemicals on the face of the earth and is very insoluble in water. However, under the right conditions of temperature and pressure, some does go into solution. As the hot water flows downslope from the silica-charged springs, it cools and the silica comes out of solution to form a series of terraces and coffer dams, behind which the cooling water ponds back. Sinter, or rock opal, is white in its pure state; however, all sorts of other chemicals are often present in the water and these add a variety of colours, both to the sinter and the terraces: antimony orange, ferrous iron green, sulphur yellow and grey. The latter two tell us something of another very special feature of the water, as does the smell of rotten eggs that pervades much of the area. (The locals don't notice the smell — they've got olfactory fatigue.) The smell comes from the volcanic gas hydrogen sulphide, a heavier-than-air and hence ground-hugging gas which reacts with oxygen to form sulphuric acid: shades of modern-day acid rain! In the same way, ferrous iron reacts with dissolved oxygen to form rust-red ferric iron oxides. So it is obvious that much of the water that boils, bubbles and hisses up from the geothermal vents is devoid of oxygen, the gas on which all air-breathers totally depend.

Back in the heyday of Victoriana, when tourists came by boat and real horse power to visit the wonders of Rotorua, sinter formed one of the great attractions of the area. The fabled Pink and White Terraces, listed among the eight natural wonders of the world, were situated on the shores of Lake Rotomahana. The Pink Terraces, coloured by ferric iron, were the warmest: they measured more than fifty metres across at the top and were called Otukapurangi (fountain of the clouded sky) by the Maori. The White Terraces were much cooler and covered an area of three hectares. Both were destroyed and submerged by an eruption on 10 June 1886, when all hell burst out over a line extending from Mount Tarawera to Waimangu, a distance of some twenty kilometres.

Some idea of the fascination of these enormous sinter cascades can be obtained by visiting the Primrose Terraces at Waiotapu, where a mere fifty centimetres of rock opal have been laid down in just 900 years.

Above 94°C, it would appear that no living organisms can exist, and the changing colours of the water and sinter are brought about entirely by physico-chemical reactions. The white opalescence of sinter, stained green by ferrous iron, turns pink in the ferric form until diluted by a flush of sulphur-charged water — an ever-changing palette of chemical colour. Wherever superheated or near-boiling water pulses to the surface, we catch a glimpse of the world as it was more than 3.6 eons ago.

The world was then a very different place, a planet devoid of life, spinning its own time-scale of day and night, lunar month and calendar year through space, with nothing to mark their progress or colour the seasons save the monochrome of ice and liquid water. Warmed by the atomic power plant of an embryonic sun, the earth received only a quarter of its present-day input of energy. The atmosphere was, how-

The White Terrace — a sinter-lating view — oil painting by Charles Blomfield.
PRIVATE COLLECTION, MASTERTON
PHOTO: THE BATH HOUSE, ROTORUA ART AND HISTORY MUSEUM

The Warbrick Terrace, Waimangu Valley, near Rotorua.

Mount Tarawera with the rift from the 1886 blow-out, part of the line of fire.

The steaming cliffs of Lake Rotomahana, above the now-submerged Pink and White Terraces.

ever, charged with carbon dioxide, water vapour and ammonia, three 'greenhouse' gases, so called because they let the heat-ray end of the sunshine in to warm the surface of both land and sea, and yet they do not let the reflected heat of earthshine back out again. At that time, too, the oceans were laden with ferrous iron and other elements and compounds which only remain in solution in their reduced state; for then, no free oxygen moved over the face of the earth.

This is not the place to rekindle the debate on the origins of life — did it fall or was it pushed? This book is in fact a celebration of the success of what we might call the process of creative evolution.

We have rock-hard evidence — fossils proving that there were life forms on earth 3.6 eons ago. So perfect is their state of preservation that we can match them with their modern living counterparts: is it too provocative to say descendants? We can label them as prokaryotes, simple bacteria-like cells. Indeed, some of these earliest denizens of the earth have been caught fossilised in the act of procreation, one cell dividing to make two new individuals.

With the correct gear and a good optical microscope, you can discover similar contemporary facts of life, happy happenings taking place in the hottest tubs of the thermal areas. However, in order to ascertain their presence and their caloric ecology, all you really need is an appreciation of colour and temperature. Eyes must suffice, for the water is very hot. They are dangerous places!

As a rule of scalded forefinger (a thermometer makes it more accurate), at temperatures too hot to hold — between 94 and 74°C — a mixture of two types of prokaryotes may be found, wefts of billions of tiny cells, grey in colour and spongy to the touch. Some obtain their energy of life by the simple oxidation of chemicals like ferrous iron, hydrogen sulphide and methane. Others use organic chemicals — simple sugars and amino acids — as their food source. These may well be the dead remains of the other types of organisms living in the sponge, or, in the thermal areas, they may have been washed in from round about 3.6 eons ago: in the absence of oxygen, many such chemicals produced by volcanic heat and pressure, lightning strikes and the like would have accumulated in seas and silts and muds. Then along came the first scavenging organisms and seized their opportunity as the world's first refuse-disposal operatives and recyclers of organic products. The decomposers were here first, and will be here at the end!

'Organic' simply means chemicals with a backbone of the element carbon, and the universal source of the carbon is and was the greenhouse gas carbon dioxide. So the process was set in motion, slowly at first, but speeding throughout time — a process that would remove carbon dioxide from the atmosphere, storing it in structured organic form.

Look in wonder at your reflection in the mirror. You are made of organic chemicals, each with a backbone of carbon borrowed from the atmosphere. Look in wonder at those patterns of colour and texture painted by other simpler forms of life, parallel to the flow of boiling water across the gradient of heat. Where water flows from a single source, the pattern is more striking, a chevron of colours as the water cools downslope. At temperatures greater than 94°, in the middle of the V, it is too hot for any form of life. Then there is the grey-pink chevron of the first zone of prokaryotes, framed by other cooler colours. Below 74° it appears cool enough for one of the most important chemicals on earth to be able to survive in working order. This is chlorophyll, the chemical switch which turned the world on to using sunlight as a source of living energy.

If you are lucky, you can catch a photograph of a rainbow in the steam above one of the hot springs. And there you have it — an all-action technicolour picture of the world on the brink of a vital breakthrough: red, orange, yellow, green, blue, indigo and violet, the colours of the rainbow. If an object like pure sinter reflects all of these colours, it will appear white. If it absorbs some, say violet, blue and red, it will appear green, as does the pigment chlorophyll. Chlorophyll is a chemical with the unique ability of passing the sun's energy on so that it can be stored in chemical form: organic chemicals such as carbohydrates, fats and protein. All the things listed on and presumably contained inside your packet of fast food are put there by kind permission of chlorophyll *a*, which is contained in leaves from all kinds of plants the world over.

Long before there were leaves, much simpler photosynthesisers did the job with great efficiency; and they are still at it around Rotorua, living it up in the hot water.

In the next temperature zone, that is, below 74° — still too hot for fingertips — the simplest light-guzzling organisms can be seen, a spongy intermix of purples, pinks, oranges and lurid greens. The range of colours is due to 'accessory' or 'helper' pigments. These, as their colours tell us, absorb other wavelengths of light energy, passing it on to the all-important chlorophyll green. In the purple and the green sulphur bacteria, the chlorophyll transforms the energy to break down hydrogen sulphide. The products of this photosynthesis are carbon dioxide, stored in organic form, and elemental sulphur, released as a by-product. The purple non-sulphur bacteria do the same, but make use of simple organic molecules rather than sulphides of hydrogen.

Only the lurid blue-green cyanobacteria contain chlorophyll *a*, the pigment that drives the bulk of the modern photosynthetic world, and only they use water as a raw material and release oxygen as a by-product. You can, in fact, see the bubbles of oxygen sitting on top of the living sandwich of bacteria which frames the flowing hot water. Silver bubbles erupt from the cyanobacteria, below which, in shade lit by the redder light that penetrates the blue-green waving filaments, are other bacteria absorbing exactly those wavelengths required to do their own photosynthetic thing, producing more life chemicals and sulphur as they grow in their oxygen-free environment. If that were all that happened, these bacterial mats would simply get thicker and thicker; but suffused throughout this living sandwich are other bacteria, which feed in darkness on the organic products producing methane — marsh gas or after-damp. Methane is an inflammable gas, feared by coal miners and other people who tunnel in the earth, and by public health engineers faced with the problem of getting rid of the contents of the dustbins of our modern effluent society. Our underground rubbish tips are producing methane in vast quantities — with explosive results for nearby householders. In the deep past of Moa's Ark, free oxygen and methane were pouring out from expansive mats of photosynthetic bacteria, which then covered vast areas of the new living world.

Cyanobacteria in hot water (about 70°C) at Waimangu.

The Waimangu Stream with hot springs, showing zonation of many life forms.

Today, the hotspots of prokaryotic life are very small, confined to temperatures above 60°C, for when the water cools below this level more aggressive forms of life, like browsing insects, crowd out and even consume the bacterial sandwich. Take a long look along the hot waterways and you will see the outer zones soon give way to crowded communities of mosses and liverworts, with even the odd 'bonsai' kanuka turning up its rootlets out of the way of the hot water in the mat below. What is even more fascinating, with a doctor's stethoscope (better than boiling your ears) you can listen to the gnashing of millions of tiny animal mouthparts as they chew their way through the crop of bacteria. None of these more complex living things can exist at higher temperatures, and all require free oxygen.

Back in Archaean time, 3.6 to 2.5 eons ago, no such things existed and the bacteria grew in abundance right across the temperature range of life from 97°C down to almost frozen solid.

So it was that for many millions of years the world was ruled by bacteria which helped to change the environment for the benefit of life. Back in those far-off days, the earth was warmed by a sun the strength of which was increasing all the time. Yet all the evidence suggests that the surface temperature of the earth showed no major increase, remaining at an equitable tropical 37°. With all those greenhouse gases about, why didn't it go on heating up?

Well, one theory suggests that all the activity of the photosynthetic bacteria slowly but surely reduced the amount of carbon dioxide present in the atmosphere: the methane released, being much more reactive, did not fully compensate for the loss of carbon dioxide. It may seem a wildly impossible hypothesis, but we do know that around 2.2 eons ago, the temperature of the earth's surface fell enough for large sections of the globe to be covered with sheets of ice. At the same time, free oxygen became abundant in the atmosphere and life on earth would never be the same again.

Photosynthesis ruled, OK? The atmospheric gases, such as oxygen, ozone, carbon dioxide, hydrogen, sulphide and methane, were pulled into living balance and kept in line by the combined activity of the earth's living skin, the developing biosphere on which we now depend.

So the geysers and hot springs of New Zealand's number one tourist hotspot give us our first 'window' into the deep past, not only of Moa's Ark, but of the heritage of the living world: a steam-driven circus of early life, which could have been shut down just because too many human beings began to tap into the thermal resource. It provided a good, non-polluting source of power, so down went the private bore-holes and up came the steam: cheap energy on tap! The only trouble was that the source of power, though spectacular, is finite; eventually, geysers stopped gushing, springs stopped bubbling and mud pools slowed their slurping, to the detriment of tour operators and hoteliers alike. Only swift action saved the day. Unpopular legislation closed the private bores, and already the great geyser called Wairoa is on the boil again and the hotels are refilling. But is it enough to save that ultimate experience of the tourist flying circus — a ride in the Tiger Moth? The old aeroplane and its partner are in good health, but landing fees at the airport have climbed so high as to threaten the economic viability of the enterprise. What of the future? Well, that is the story of Moa's Ark.

Milford Sound

The Milford Track takes you through some of the finest unspoilt temperate rain forest and mountain scenery to be found in the world. Served by fine mountain huts, it provides visitors each year with a glimpse of Fiordland, itself the heart of 1.25 million hectares of World Heritage site. The World Heritage label brackets it with Mount Everest, Yellowstone, the Egyptian Pyramids and the Taj Mahal: key tourist resources which now have international appeal and protection. No wonder the visitors flood in, despite the background sound of falling water. Seven thousand millimetres of rain fall in an average year — enough to drown a four-storey building. That all this water does not stay in the one place is due to the steepness of the mountains which, in places, rise direct out of the sea, peaking at 2,700 metres.

So it is possible to experience waterfalls cascading down from a dizzy height directly into Milford Sound, and many people do so from the deck of a tour boat. Tourists come in coachloads, about 80,000 each year, from Queenstown and beyond to cruise the calm, land-locked waters and, if brave enough, to take a cold, high-impact shower right on the foredeck.

There are five sorts of water in Fiordland: ice, rain, high-impulse, soak-away and salty sea.

Ice, frozen water hard as rock, ground out the glaciated fiords and shaped the land, then retreated to the higher ground. Rainwater, slighty acid (as it always is), blows in pure and untainted, having left its salt behind in the Tasman Sea. High-impulse, free-fall waterfalls, tumbling off bare rock down into the sea, comprise crystal-clear water full of oxygen and bubbles.

Soak-away water descends in a more leisurely fashion. Supplying the local vegetation en route, the surplus suffuses its way through the humus-rich peats and soils to emerge honey-gold brown. This is a tincture of history, for all the humic chemicals making up this wonderful colour were produced by plants that have grown on the catchment in the past — plants of mountain, pasture, swamp, bog, grassland and forest, whose roots have bound the soil onto the mountainsides and the foliage of which provided shelter and succour for the whole cross-section of animal life, including the great birds that gave Moa's Ark its name. In places the natural hold-all capacity of the roots is not sufficient for the task. Storms, rapid snow-melt and earthquake cause the vegetation to slip away, creating a tattered fetlock around the feet of the now bare slopes. The clear waters are muddied for a while with silt and soil as the whole living system, complete with trunks, slips into the fiord.

The fifth type of water is, of course, the sea, suffused with salt. In large amounts it is toxic to most forms of land-based life, but when it is too dilute it spells sweet-water doom for most organisms of the sea.

Moa's Ark

It is the intermix between these five types of water which gives Fiordland its most mysterious aspect and us our next window into the past. Here we can look into a shadowy underworld full of Palaeozoic treasures of 600 million years ago, when life on the land was still based on those not-so-simple bacterial mats to which had been added a growing diversity of more complex plants, made of true cells, that are best called algae. Beneath and between the tides, complex communities of these early life forms laid down deposits of limestone, building large, readily fossilisable structures called stromatolites. Together these organisms formed gigantic reefs, whose weight may well have been enough to depress the crust of the earth, tilting islands and even continents. The upward growth of the reef might then have matched the sinking of the land — as it does in modern coral reefs — enough to keep the heads of the photosynthetic communities within their optimum (one is almost tempted to say 'chosen') environment between the tides. James Lovelock, whose Gaia hypothesis has recently done so much to make people believe in and cherish

Four of the five sorts of water in Milford Sound.
KEN MILLER

the living earth, also suggests that the weight of these reefs, combined with inshore sediments, could have tipped the balance of the earth's crustal plates, and not the continents drifting on their way across the face of the globe.

Something must have happened to send Moa's Ark on its way, for 600 million years ago this particular piece of crustal real estate was situated in the temperate zone of the Northern Hemisphere. It was then part of a shallow sea dotted with volcanic islands set on the margin of the great continent Gondwana, which included in its compass the prototypes of most of the land masses now found in the Southern Hemisphere — Australia, Antarctica, India, southern Africa and America.

Science fiction? No, science fact. The story is there in the rocks, embedded in their magnetic and solid-state memory banks, there for geologists and rock hounds to read.

New Zealand rocks that tell this part of the story are found on the west coast of the South Island at Charleston, and in the Victoria Range near aptly named Reefton. Although these rocks contain no recognisable fossils, we know from fossils of the same age elsewhere that by this time in the earth's history many animals of very different types were living in the sea. The fantastic fact is that some of them, or at least their direct descendants, are still living it up down in Fiordland.

One of the most spectacular animals living in the waters of the fiords is a wonderful sea pen, which glories in the name *Sarcophyllum bollonsi*. Sea pens are so called because they bear more than a passing resemblance to a quill pen, the like of which might have been used by Mr Pickwick. They are members of the great group of animals that includes jellyfish, anemones and corals, the prototypes of which were doing well in the seas 600 million years ago.

Another group present then, and still found in Fiordland waters, are the lamp shells, or brachiopods. Find their shells on the beach but do not be fooled, they are not related to our modern-day mussels and oysters. The giveaway comes when you look at the larger lower shell, which is pierced by a hole just like the wick hole in a Roman oil lamp. When the brachiopod is alive, the hole is filled not by a wick but by a stalk which holds the animal down onto a rock or another shell.

On a world scale, fossil lamp shells are abundant, for they were once the shelled rulers of the waves. Lamp shells 'alive alive oh' are a much rarer phenomenon, and to meet one face to face must be the dream of every budding zoologist. It's no easy matter, for many lamp shells seem to thrive in those dark recesses of the sea untouched by wave action or temperature fluctuation, and they are therefore usually found in water too deep for even the most highly trained scuba diver. But in places like southern New Zealand, thanks to the mixing of the five types of water, they live not far below the surface. You can even find them in Wellington Harbour!

Fresh water is less dense than sea water, so it floats on the salty sea. In the inner recesses of the fiords, where wave action is as rare as a dry day, the sweet water can form a layer on the surface up to ten metres deep. It provides a region of honey gold which acts as a filter. The sweet water absorbs the light rays and the scene rapidly darkens with depth. When diving, it is a confusing experience unless you know what is happening. In relatively shallow water, it creates an eternal twilight, which allows the diver to peep into the deep past.

Thanks to reduced light levels, coral trees grow at diveable level in the fiords.
KIM WESTERSKOV

One of the most sought-after animals of the Sounds is the black coral, *Antipathes aperta*. Like the lamp shells and sea pens, it may be found here in shallow water just beneath the sweet-water light lock. In Fiordland the black coral is a protected species, and the diver may only take pictures. Growing like bushes up to two metres tall, these colonial animals form an efficient net which enables them to catch and feed on the plankton as it floats past. So efficient is the net that it also collects all sorts of other suspended material and can only thrive in the cleanest water free of sediments. It's little wonder this coral grows so well in Fiordland's limpid waters, where it creates an underwater forest of sombre beauty.

The side branches of some of the coral trees are decorated with what at first sight look like red and white striped worms. Closer inspection reveals that they are the fifty-centimetre-long arms of the long-armed snake brittle star, *Astrobrachion constrictum*, a relative of the starfish and sea urchins. What are these animals doing, wrapped in such a tight embrace?

In a night-time dive the puzzle comes alive. The snake star's arms unwind and the animal begins browsing along the branches, not eating the black coral but feeding on protein-rich slime which the coral exudes.

During some recent studies on black coral, a very rare drought occurred in Milford Sound, leading to the almost complete disappearance of the golden-brown freshwater layer. The result was more light and a heavy 'bloom' of planktonic plants, so dense that they smothered and killed many of the corals. Some of those with snake stars in their branches were cleansed of the clogging plankton by their browsing partners and so survived. Study of coral colonies near land slips showed that the browsing action of snake stars cleaned away the clinging sediment and the corals survived here too — a wonderful example of mutual help, or symbiosis. One can only surmise when such relationships developed in the past. Certainly back in those times before there were any plants to protect the land surface from erosion, self-cleansing subaquatic systems must have been the signal of success.

Exploration of the fiords, whose glaciated sides fall sheer to depths in excess of 300 metres, is in its infancy, so what treasures are there still in store? Perhaps one day an underwater viewing platform or even a fleet of passenger submarines will allow the tourist to see all this and much more at first hand. Until then patience, well laced with films and videos, must suffice.

In recent years plans were laid to turn the sweet waters of Fiordland into export gold. Thirsty nations who treasure fresh water much more than the fossil fuel they export from their parched lands wanted to tap into the essence of the Sounds. All sorts of schemes were proposed to minimise the likelihood of oil spills and pollution, but eventually the whole plan was embargoed until sufficient research had been carried out on this unique environment. We need to ensure that the delicate balance of that shadowy world where the five waters mix remains intact. Six hundred million years of history is a natural heritage too valuable to destroy.

WINDOW 3

Poor Knights

The main pulse of life was to remain locked in the sea for more than 300 million years, protected from too rapid environmental change by the constant presence of salty water. A whole panoply of invertebrate life forms, animals without backbones, came into being, some testing their land legs between tides, on rock, shingle, sand and silt of shores and estuaries.

In the short term, the flow of materials eroded from the land into the sea, be they organic or mineral, is a one-way ticket. Once there, they enrich the surface waters, causing algal blooms and speeding the growth of reefs and the continual rain of sediment down into the abyss.

However, in the long term, movements of the earth's crust, especially when on the scale of drifting continents, cause all sorts of tensions, depressions and upliftings. Land masses are cleaved to form new oceans, and the beds of old seas are thrust up, forming new mountain chains of limestone, mudstone and shale, all ready to be recycled again. The ponderous cycles of geologic change grind on, reshaping the face of the globe.

Back around 570 million years ago, it would appear that things were beginning to settle down a bit. Many of the rocks laid down after this record no sign of glaciation, so either all the land masses and their reef-forming fringes had drifted out of the grip of the polar circles, or the greenhouse gases were in some new, high-Regulo balance with the improving power of the sun. It was probably a bit of both.

Certainly by that time there was an abundance of oxygen free in the atmosphere and dissolved in the sea. Worldwide photosynthesis had done a good job, opening up the potentialities of life energy derived from the sun, now made readily available through processes of oxidation.

To prove it, the rocks laid down at this time are full of fossils, as we see with the ancient limestones found around Nelson. They include lamp shells, two-valved molluscs, trilobites — that is, animals with jointed legs related to crabs, crayfish and insects — and the remains of what appear to be the teeth or gill rakers of soft-bodied lampreys. Other rocks of this age (known as the Cambrian period) include the remains of spiny-skinned animals related to our modern sea urchins, and the frail imprint of jellyfish and, later, the unmistakable remains of corals.

In that period, New Zealand was situated in the north temperate zone, but it was on the move towards warmer waters. Our window onto this shadowy underwater world opens in the subtropical waters of the east coast of Northland — sailing waters par excellence.

The Poor Knights themselves provide the world with some of its most spectacular dive sites, and also with the wise counsel of Wade Doak. Wade is a diver of international repute whose contact with the wonder and abundance of life around these islands has made him one of the champions of marine conservation. He lives on the mainland, on an organic-based orchard full of fruits of both temperate and tropical climes, all set about with regenerating native bush. From here he leads expeditions — scientific and tourist — to view the abundant mix of life in these waters, giving us a taste of life from the deep past of Moa's Ark.

A good dive starts within the magnificence of the kelp forests surrounded by giant brown seaweeds, which are so typical of temperate waters. Grazed by sea urchins and bejewelled with sea and cushion stars, these forests provide shelter and nursery grounds for many fish. Below them stretch the sponge gardens arrayed with animals, many of which look so much like plants that early biologists placed them in that group: worms, moss animals, sea firs, anemones, sea mats, molluscs and encrusting red seaweeds. Each is fixed to its own appointed spot until plucked off or pruned by one of the local gardeners. Around the Poor Knights, the head gardener is, without doubt, the leather jacket. This ultra-territorial trigger fish constantly browses, weeding out individual specimens and opening up new rock for recolonisation.

Such gardens present an ever-changing pattern of life so long as new generations of all the plants and animals are in the offing. Fortunately, most of the garden animals produce plenty of progeny in the form of free-floating larvae which drift with the plankton, far and wide, to seed new locations and fill vacant niches. When the larger territorial animals like the trigger fish are removed, the same is not true. The niche may remain open and the post of head gardener may never be refilled; adverse changes begin to take place and the dynamic balance of the gardens and the forests may be destroyed.

For this reason, overfishing — and especially spearfishing for the largest trophy specimens — wreaks havoc in these inshore waters. This is one reason why pressure was brought to bear, and the case was won, to make Poor Knights a marine reserve. The rule is no nets, lines or hooks: leave only ripples; take only pictures. The reserve is working, and it is working a miracle.

Dive with Wade Doak in this, his own home patch, and once across the reserve boundary you will see the sea explode with fish. It is almost like swimming through the wall of an aquarium tank. What is even more rare and exciting is that the fish are unafraid of your human presence, they take you, the bubble-blowing visitor, to be no more than part of the local scene. You do not even need to don an aqualung — a snorkel and mask can be your window into this wonderland.

With Poor Knights and the mainland Goat Island Reserve to hand, marine science is beginning to make some important discoveries. For instance, it is now known that the prize specimens, the largest grandparent fish and crayfish, are of extreme importance in these communities. They are by far the greatest producers of fertile spawn, and it is their excess production that bolsters the local populations, allowing spillover and the restocking of nearby waters. There is already ample proof that marine reserves not only benefit marine science and tourism, but also local inshore fisheries. When the Poor Knights initiative has spawned a series of reserves all around the coast of Moa's Ark, we can all look forward to richer days ahead.

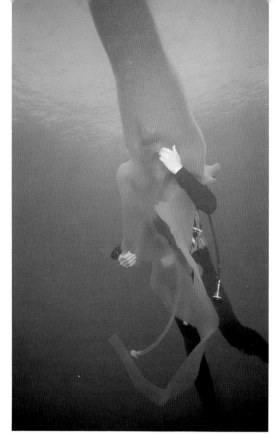

Giant salp and diver.
WADE DOAK

Before we draw a curtain over this window on the past, mention must be made of two other groups of animals. Throughout the Cambrian and the next 200 million years, Moa's Ark was drifting through tropical waters into the Southern Hemisphere. It was a time that saw the development of great reefs, formed of stony corals. There are no coral reefs around the Poor Knights, but solitary stony corals are there in abundance, now that the no-take ethic is in place.

The other group of note are the tunic animals, a group that includes the sea squirts, abundant members of most inshore water communities; and one of the most amazing creatures to be found around New Zealand, the giant salp — a rare but very exciting dive buddy off the Poor Knights.

Most tunic animals are small, semi-transparent, bag-like creatures which, when pressed, squirt out a stream of salt water. Many sea squirts are attached to seaweeds or rocks, and provide advanced diversity within sponge gardens and kelp forests alike. The salps, though members of the same group, are free-floating colonial animals, and the waters around the Poor Knights boast the largest salps in the world. A giant salp, up to thirty metres long, appears to be no more than a transparent sack: you can put your arm or even your head inside. But have a care, for they tear very easily, and their simple transparency hides a very special secret. Study of the life cycle of these creatures has shown that they are members of a group called the chordates, for in their larval stages they possess a prototype backbone, a step along the road to life on land and a sign of the changing geological times.

Goatfish (red mullet), *Upeneichthys porosus*, and sponge garden in the Poor Knights Marine Reserve.
WADE DOAK

Tongariro Records

My favourite groups of plants are the mosses and the liverworts. My reasons for making this choice are many, but revolve around the facts that there are not too many of them (only about 20,000 on a world scale), and thus not too many names to learn; they are also good indicators of the environment, so they tell you a lot about the place; and they are always there, spring, summer, autumn and winter, waiting to be identified.

My favourite place in New Zealand is Tongariro, sacred to the Maori people and gifted by the chief Te Heu Heu Tukino to become New Zealand's first national park in 1894. Some argue it was one of the first in the world, for it was originally gifted in 1887, soon after Yellowstone was established in North America. A fabulous volcano, Tongariro was the first place in which I saw the world's largest moss and the largest leafy liverwort.

We do not know exactly where or when the world's first moss or liverwort grew on earth, but all indications would point to a damp, subtropical area around 400 million years ago. New Zealand would have fitted the bill, for about the end of the Silurian period its bit of the earth's crust was edging down across 30°S and the Tuhua mountain-building phase, which would raise Moa's Ark above water level, was in the offing.

Mosses and liverworts are, without doubt, plants of the land. They produce capsules containing spores which are able to withstand dessication for long periods of time. When the spores arrive, blown to a suitable damp spot, they germinate to form a plant that is able to turn itself on and off as the environment demands. Under water stress they shut up shop, curling and shrivelling. Although in appearance they are translucent and delicate-looking, the structure of their cells prevents collapse and damage of the living contents. So, as soon as rain or mist drifts in again, they can unroll and get on with the job of photosynthesis and the completion of their life cycle. Mosses and liverworts do it in the wet, and their organs of reproduction produce static eggs and mobile sperm. The latter must be able to swim to fertilise the egg, and they do so through the surface film of water: the 'deep end' for them is a tenth of a millimetre of water. Each new embryo has the ability to grow, not into another moss or liverwort plant, but into a stalked capsule full of spores, each one ready to start the whole cycle off again.

The largest moss in the world is *Dawsonia superba*, and it can grow up to half a metre tall, complete with a large, flattened, tufted, egg-shaped capsule on top. Inside the wiry stem is a central core of stiffening cells, which are somewhat longer than broad, like the woody cells of higher plants. It has been shown that these cells help to transport water up the stem, but not out to the leaves, for there is no

The summits of Tongariro, Ngauruhoe
and Ruapehu from the north.
CRAIG POTTON

The largest moss in the world,
Dawsonia superba.

The world's largest thallose liverwort, *Monoclea forsteri.*

connection to the midrib of the leaf. In consequence, as soon as the air gets too dry, the leaves wilt and curl up round the stem. Suck one, and you will see them unfurl. The leaves are arranged in a spiral fashion around the stem — a trademark of the mosses.

The largest liverwort in the world is *Monoclea forsteri*, a great, flat, shiny plant, each lobe making the whole thing look not unlike a human liver, up to twenty centimetres long and five broad. They grow on dripping rocks and near waterfalls, where it is rarely, if ever, too dry. True liverworts do not have leaves, the whole liver-like mass being called a thallus.

Leafy liverworts — and under the lens or microscope they are among the most delicately beautiful land plants — do have leaves, arranged in two rows down either side of the stem. There may be a third row of smaller leaves on the underside, but the leaves are never spirally arranged. The largest leafy liverwort in the world is *Plagiochila*, with stems up to thirty centimetres long.

Because individual mosses and liverworts are not semi-permanent landscape features, like trees, it is impossible to say with certainty exactly where the biggest is at any one time. They propagate, grow up to record dimensions and then rot away, having released the spores ready for another crack at a Guinness gold.

In order to see these mini-monsters, all you need do is walk along the many tracks and trails through the forests which climb the flanks of Tongariro, and keep your eyes at ground level. If you decide to be a judge and measure the contestants, please be careful where you put your knees, feet, hands and tripod legs: it would be unfair to flatten another aspiring champion.

Moss field, *Rhacomitrium*, near Mount Ruapehu.

One of the world's largest leafy liverworts, *Schistochila* sp.

As you stand up again you are also likely to meet another world champion face to face: *Ephemeropsis trentepohlioides* — an orange weft covering the twigs above, and one of the world's smallest mosses. You will need a lens to see the tiny capsules rising from an orange mat complete with a ring of minute leaves at the base.

Back in the Silurian period, there were no trees to provide either a podium or shelter from the sun and wind for ancestors of these record-breakers. So the first of these fascinating plants must have grown in wet, dripping places, near streams and waterfalls, where they still make their presence felt today.

A climb up to the top of Tongariro not only gets my botanical records all of a twitch, it also makes me feel very much at home, for en route, I pass many mosses and liverworts which also grow in England. *Andreaea rupestris* is common on bare mountain rocks across the world, dark black in colour to protect its delicate chlorophyll from too much light. The grey, furry-when-wet lambswool moss is also very widespread in such habitats, and appears to enjoy living on bare lava.

Others, such as *Tetradontium brownianum*, are rare, being found only on mountains in Europe, North America and New Zealand and nowhere in between. Could it be a case of intercontinental spore dispersal? Tough things, spores, for they have been found floating in the cold of the upper atmosphere, ready to drop in. The spores of mosses and leafy liverworts, preserved dry in little packets for years, have been revived and have started to grow again. And all of this despite the fact that their leaves are only one cell thick! The plant kingdom was going to have to do a lot better than that if it was really to conquer living on the land.

Rangitoto Brinkmanship

More than a third of the whole population of New Zealand live amongst the remains of fifty volcanoes. Extinct these volcanoes may be, but the volcanic field is far from dead and a new vent may pop up at any time. Metropolitan Auckland lies astride the line of fire which stretches beyond Rumble III, bubbling away on the floor of the Pacific, south to Ruapehu and a little beyond, with some spectacular views of activity en route. New Zealand itself is one end of the huge arc of fire stretching from the North Island volcanoes to the central Pacific.

The last time there was a major eruption within the city limits was around AD 1220, with a lesser burst of activity only 200 years ago. Maori people left their footprints in the volcanic ash of this particular time, which fell on their island home just next door to the new volcano, Rangitoto.

Today, you can get there by air or sea, and both approaches have much to recommend them. My favourite is the former, for it gives an overview of the place, crater and all, and a chance to ride in another remarkable flying machine, a Grumman Goose. This 1940s-type plane, all aluminium and unclad geodesics, is able to both take off and land in the sea. It can then trundle up the beach, providing both pilot and passengers a dry landing.

A Grumman Goose waddles up the beach.

Rangitoto Island from the south.

The island's most recent cone of basalt sits symmetrically inside a larger one, which has been partly destroyed. It is well worth making both the ascent and the descent into the crater in order to see it all for yourself. There are signposted tracks and nature trails to lead you there through the flows of jagged scoria, irregular lumps of lava pitted with gas bubbles, almost as if they had just come off the boil.

From the highest point there is a good view of the Auckland skyline, complete with mirror-glass high-rise, and the drop into the crater provides shelter from the wind and a chance to reflect on the next eruption. The experts would suggest that you are standing in the safest place, for it is unlikely that a new volcano will arise in the same spot. But experts can be wrong, so you stand straining your ears and your imagination for any tell-tale sound. The scrape of falling rock makes your hair stand on end, but it's only another tourist dropping in. On a hot day, and this is subtropical Auckland, the surface of the bare black lava gets very hot indeed and the illusion of renewed activity shimmers all around, distorting the view through your lens.

The most amazing feature of Rangitoto is that between the bare and apparently barren lava flows are great strands and stands of forest. The dominant pohutukawa stay dull green for most of the year, but in December, New Zealand's Christmas tree puts on its chauvinistic show of red stamens (the male part of the flower). Glossy green leaves of puka provide contrast; together the two provide a sheltered habitat for some 200 native species of plants that have made this their home in the last 200 years, recolonising after the last eruption.

Flowers of the pohutukawa tree,
Metrosideros excelsa.

Pohutukawa trees growing out of volcanic
scoria, Rangitoto Island.

Moa's Ark

Just how the great trees found their first roothold is anyone's guess, but there they are, gnarled trunks twisting up and equally gnarled roots twisting down to find water and nutrients among the tumbled blocks. However, once established (and it was in recent time, for photographs taken in the 1870s show a wilderness of bare rock with little large vegetation) their presence has the effect not only of casting shade and providing shelter but of adding organic matter, leaves and twigs, to fill the cracks and crevices and cap the bare rocks. So much so that great clumps of tufting lillies are found living it up down on the ground, as well as perching on the branches of the trees where they usually belong. Perching plants have the ability to create their own soil, grabbing all the water they need as it flows down the trunks of their supporters. Nature's own hydroponic culture here on Rangitoto has moved down to ground level, where the correct term could perhaps be rockoponics.

One trail all visitors like to take leads them through the deep shade of Kidney Fern Gulch, so called because its dark recesses simply drip with kidney ferns. Of all the New Zealand ferns, this would appear to have the most delicate leaves. Wide, almost transparent, and lined with veins, they look as if the first whiff of drought would kill them off. They are, however, much tougher than they look. Made up of many cells, they can control water loss, and the veins help keep them well supplied. They also keep the black sporangia well supplied, for, like mosses and liverworts, ferns and their kin also produce spores, not in tiny capsules, but on their leaves.

Path through kidney-fern glade in pohutukawa forest.

These true ferns came along much later in our story, so to find our next window onto the past we must look among the larger blocks for a much more insignificant plant, a plant the like of which first grew on earth around 400 million years ago. Its name: *Psilotum*. This was a time when all the continents of the world were drifting together in one great land mass called Pangaea, well before the split into Gondwana, the southern continent, and Laurasia, the northern continent. New Zealand was just beginning to rise from the sea at about 30°S, and there were major glaciations scraping away at the rocks of Brazil, for South America then lay astride the South Pole.

Although some argue that *Psilotum* is a highly specialised whisk fern of more recent origin, others point to fossils of great age which resemble it in many ways. It has bare stems, its branches always dividing, like those of seaweeds, into two distinct halves. Tiny, scale-like things are all it has for leaves. The stems, however, are green, photosynthetic, and have pores that can close and slow down water loss. Inside each stem are stiff rods of elongated 'woody' cells, which provide support and help pipe in a supply of water right up to the tip of the stem and to the sporangia. The sporangia contain the 'I don't care too much about drought' spores, which, once released, carry the message of successful life far and wide. *Psilotum* is also found growing as far north as Spain, and similar ancestral plants once grew in Scotland.

Once the spores have landed in a suitably damp crack in the rocks, they germinate to form a very different sort of plant, an underground scrap of a thing called a prothallus. Having no resemblance to its parent, it does bear the organs of sexual reproduction, but like the mosses and liverworts, whisk ferns can only do it in the wet. Once the sperms have swum and fertilised the eggs, up pops a new *Psilotum* plant to start the whole life-cycle off again. This dual existence of under-water sex and flamboyant spore-bearers was the key that allowed the plant kingdom to take this next step up towards life on the land. It was an immense step for creative evolution, and how it came about we can only surmise.

Psilotum nudum.

Lichens encrusting rocks under a pohutukawa.

The bare and not-so-bare rocks of Rangitoto are also home to a number of plants and animals which at least hint how land legs led to the dry-shod real estate. Lichens are present in abundance, some almost hidden in tiny self-excavated pits in the rock; others, dark green, orange and black, encrust the surface, while *Cladia*, like stiff white lace, festoons the rockeries. Lichens are two-faced, for they are made up of two types of plants, an alga and a fungus. The algae may be simple blue-greens, related to those prokaryotes back in the Precambrian, or they may be more advanced true cells related to the modern-day seaweeds. They are photosynthetic and feed the lichen. Fungi related to toadstools, moulds and mushrooms are decomposers, living off the leftovers of others; they form the substance of the lichen, giving it both shape and form. Together, they make an unbeatable twosome, the one providing sustenance through photosynthesis, the other a home base and a launch pad for the spores.

Down beside the sea the most abundant seaweed is Venus's necklace. Like *Psilotum*, it branches always into two equal halves in a dichotomous way, but it can only stand upright when supported by the water. Once the tide is out, it lies flat on its back. The large seaweeds grow attached to, not rooted into, the rocks, while the dark crevices beneath provide a home for lamp shells, ready to light up the face of any passing zoologist. Two real molluscs are also common grazing amongst the seaweeds: a limpet-like creature called *Onchidella*, which has no shell, only a thick rubbery covering, for it is a sort of slug; and the handsome cat's eye snail. Both, like your garden slugs and snails, are pulmonates. If you look with care, you will be able to see a hole or operculum leading into a damp dark chamber in which there is a lung. Pulmonates are air-breathers, the shape of things to come.

46

Taranaki Futures

New Zealand's best-known mountain is probably Taranaki. An almost perfect volcano in every way, shape and form, and still on the active list (though quiet for just over 200 years), it dominates the seaside city of New Plymouth and the pages of many geography texts.

From the top of its 2,500-metre near-perfect cone you can look down on what must be the neatest national park in the world. Neat, not because of the perfection of its management nor the behaviour of its visitors, although both are of a high standard, but because of its shape — an almost complete circle. The brown of native bush and forest covering the lower slopes gives way to rich green farmland, almost as if drawn with a gigantic pair of compasses. On a clear day you can also see Ruapehu, 130 kilometres to the east, and, in the distance, the snow-capped peaks of the South Island.

It's a great tramp up to the top, two hours or so the fitness freaks say, but for a wandering botanist, and especially for fern lovers, it takes at least five glorious hours with lots of stops and things to see, time to catch your breath to help you on your way.

Enter the park by the East Egmont route along the Patea River and the friendly

Red-billed gulls, *Larus scopulinus*, on their launch pad below Mount Taranaki.

A glade of mamaku tree ferns, *Cyathea medullaris.*

Mamaku tree ferns from above.

face waving you on your way is that of a biodynamic farmer of the Rudolf Steiner school: someone who believes in putting as much into his farm as he takes out of it, and he appears to make a good healthy living out of the bargain. (This is a bargain that should be struck between every farmer and the land they hold in care.) The large yellow tank on the back of his tractor contains only home-brewed organic fertiliser, and the fuel that gives the tractor its motive power leads us to Taranaki's special window on the past. It links us to the time that spans the Carboniferous to Permian periods, 100 million years, when the rate of world photosynthesis was almost enough to take its breath away.

The Devonian period is best called the Age of the Ferns, for it was then that the ferns and their allies, the club mosses and the horsetails, took over the earth. Back in those days, many of them were built on a gigantic scale, some up to forty metres tall with trunks five metres in girth. They grew in vast swamps in which their sexual generation, small green scale-like things, could thrive. Most of these huge swamps were in tropical and subtropical climes.

When the great leaves and trunks fell to earth, they sank into the stagnant, oxygen-free water of the swamp, where they could not rot and so remained in the form of peat, layer upon layer of the stuff. These were eventually covered by rocks and, when compressed, turned into coal. The black stuff we burned in our grates and in the fireboxes of steam engines was pure fern power. It was an enormous store of the energy of the sun and a repository of carbon dioxide, removed from the atmosphere and locked up out of harm's way until technology plugged the modern world back into fern power and the problems of the greenhouse effect.

The Carboniferous period was marked by widespread glaciation across Africa, South America and India. Was it just that they then lay across the Pole and were undergoing a major phase of mountain building? Or was it that the coal swamps acted as a gigantic heat pump, pumping down the greenhouse gas into store and so bringing about a cooling of the atmosphere? In actual fact, it was probably a bit of both and we must be thankful that our local lucky star, the sun, was warming up all the time, redressing the balance.

No true Carboniferous coal is found in New Zealand, for during that period of time its climate was too cold and its steep mountains were being continuously crumpled and eroded away. The local marine record is also very poor, being found only in one locality, Kakahu in the South Island. From other places on earth we know that sharks were becoming dominant in the sea, and fish with scales and thick lobe-like fins had ventured out from the shallow water. In time, giant frogs and toads hopped about in the coal swamps. Like the ferns, these amphibians were totally dependent on fresh water for the completion of their life-cycle. The ferns and amphibians represent the two lines of advance which, by the end of this period, would have helped produce the first true land plants and animals.

In order to get some idea of what life was like in the giant fern forests, all we need do is take a walk up into those places on Taranaki where fires have run amok, destroying the native bush. There, especially in the valleys, recolonisation has been ably assisted by the mamaku, the world's largest contemporary tree fern, which may grow to more than twenty metres in height.

Walking through these glades, dwarfed by the sunshades of giant leaves, you can savour the power of plants: power to trap the energy of the sun; power to ameliorate the local climate, keeping the soil damp enough for spores to germinate, sperms to swim and embryos to grow into another leafy giant. As if to prove that it is wet enough, large dragonflies drone in, lounging about on the koru before they fly off once again to feed on other insects — one good reason to rejoice that this is the twentieth century, for 300 million years ago their counterparts had wingspans of two metres and they, too, probably fed on the wing. The insects, the real masters of the land and the first to conquer flight, were out and about at that time and were doing fine.

Koru are the trade mark of the ferns, each young leaf shaped like a bishop's crozier and covered with scales which protect the young leaflets as they unfurl. No wonder Air New Zealand chose the koru as its symbol of safety and strength, as the Maori does: a spiral of living energy rising up from the forest floor to tap the energy of the sun and to power generations to come.

The tracks that lead up beyond the fern glades take the visitor through some of the best zoned vegetation they could wish to find, each zone reflecting the environment as it changes with altitude, and each zone with its own particular ferns, ranging from the delicate filmy ferns perching on the branches, through the Prince of Wales feathers growing in the deep shade, to the crown fern, a tough plant with thicker, leathery leaves and able to grow in more open country. There too the modern club mosses are found in abundance, some as epiphytes, others growing in sunny situations in the open. The Devonian may well have been the age of the ferns, but New Zealand is one of their modern strongholds and Taranaki is a happy hunting ground for fern lovers.

At this point in our story we will tear ourselves away from the zoned gardens of botanical delight and skip back to the top of Taranaki. Binoculars at the ready! On a clear day it is possible to pick out the unmistakable form of oil rigs probing and producing from the oil and gas fields not far offshore. The rigs are built and serviced in New Plymouth, which has in recent years become something of a boom town. The fuel that now flows ashore and is doing great things for the country's balance of payments is all thanks to the excess production of plant communities of the not-so-distant past, for New Zealand's coal and oil deposits were all laid down in more recent times.

F is for fern, fossil fuels and for future. Fossil fuel is a finite resource and should be used with the care it deserves, especially when we know that its combustion is releasing all that carbon dioxide back into the atmosphere, which is now being warmed by an even hotter sun. Antarctica once again sits across the South Pole: covered in eternal ice, it is helping to keep things cool. But how eternal is that ice now the fossil fuel pumps of the world are being run in reverse?

A visitor centre explaining all this, founded by the oil industry and funded by tourism, would be a step in the right direction towards local and world understanding of the problem.

Furled fronds of the silver fern, *Cyathea dealbata*.

Unfurling fronds of the mamaku tree fern.

Drilling rig, the gas-fired power station and
ancient volcanoes.

Takitimu Leaves

T he Permian period of geological time lasted from 300 to 235 million years ago. Moa's Ark had once again sunk beneath the surface of the seas, wrecked by erosion and the continual shift of the continents. Perhaps it was all to the good, for the sinking hulk was heading down across 60° latitude towards the South Pole. The continents of Australia, Antarctica and the island of Tasmania weren't far away, and the seabed from which the Ark would eventually be rebuilt was being covered with sediments derived by erosion from the rocks of these land masses.

There is little doubt that the seas were dotted with icebergs and with volcanic islands. Plants may have grown on the islands and animals roamed; they were no longer confined to those areas around coastal and freshwater swamps. New plants with gigantic compound leaves and trunks were moving out across the land. Unlike the modern tree ferns, they did not have to grow in areas close to permanent water. Their trunks were well supported and their leaves supplied with ample water via a well-developed woody plumbing system. Sugars produced in their leaves were moved about the plant via an efficient transport system called the phloem, all well tried and tested from Devonian times onward.

Like the true ferns, their leaves bore sporangia, big (mega) ones and small (micro) ones. Apart from size, the main difference was that, although the micro-spores were released like pollen to be transported by the wind, the megaspores stayed put and, after fertilisation, developed *in situ*, protected by two scale-like leaves, into a seed full of stored energy and promise for the future.

These were the seed ferns. Seeds are survival packs within which the embryo can aestivate if it's too dry and hibernate if it's too cold: in essence they can hang on until conditions are once more right for germination.

Although seeds have become the keystone of success of all land plants, no seed ferns survive today. They came, they did their job and went to the fossil bank of extinction in the later intervals of the Cretaceous and early Permian periods.

One of the most distinctive seed ferns in the southern branch of the fossil bank goes by the name of *Glossopteris*. Unlike their cousins of the then-warmer northern lands, they had fleshy, fibrous, tongue-shaped leaves which preserved very well and are often found in great masses in deposits formed close to ice. They were evidently tough plants and could grow amongst the glaciers that partly covered Antarctica, India, South Africa, Australia and South America.

Dr Edward Wilson, scientist and artist on the ill-fated Scott expedition to the South Pole, found the leaves of this singular plant in sandstone near the infamous Beardmore Glacier: the first proof that life had existed in the past so close to the Pole. It was an exciting and crucial discovery, so Wilson dragged the heavy fossil

Fossil leaf of *Glossopteris* from the
Takitimu Mountains, collected by
J. D. Campbell.
KEN MILLER

specimens on his sledge until the expedition's last stopping place, where they were found later.

Despite its importance and widespread occurrence in the fossil record, for a long time no sign of *Glossopteris* was found in New Zealand. Some people argued that New Zealand was not part of this southern land mass of Gondwana. Others cited its peripolar position astride latitude 60°S and its volcanic origins as good reasons for the absence of any land plants, however tough.

Later, a single leaf was found in the rocks of the right age in the Takitimu Mountains, not far from Lake Manapouri in the south of the South Island. Here at last was a definite link, a leaf washed into the logbook of Moa's Ark, proving it to be part of, or at least adjacent to, the supercontinent of the southern world. A few years later, Professor Mildenhall, who made the original discovery while demonstrating this rock-lined window into the Permian world, cracked open another and another and yet another rock, each one impressing his audience with further *Glossopteris* impressions. Had they grown on the embryo Moa's Ark? Or were they rafted in on an iceberg from nearby continents? Only time will fill the gaps in our knowledge.

Moa's Ark

What the seed ferns did for the plant kingdom — building a permanent bridge onto the land — the reptiles were doing for the kingdom of the animals. Seed ferns produce seeds, reptiles produce shelled eggs, so each in their own way had done away with the restrictions of bath-time reproduction; each had their survival packs.

During the Carboniferous period, amphibians and reptiles had hopped and crawled about, making the most of the habitats on offer. The Permian saw the reptiles gain dominance; great, lumbering, armour-plated things, two and a half metres in length, but they were not the dinosaurs. The tyrant lizards came, saw and conquered much later.

At first, few reptiles ventured into Gondwana, despite the fact that there were land connections in abundance to the north. The southern lands were just too cold for these cold-blooded animals. However, as the main land masses of Gondwana began to swing away from the South Pole, the reptiles began to leave their permanent imprints across Brazil, southern Africa and northern India.

One strange group of Permian fossils, found both in the South and North Islands, are reef corals of tropical origin. Whether these were rafted in by ice, which seems unlikely, nudged in by later seafloor movements or were formed as fringing reefs around the volcanic islands during tropical interglacials at 80°S, we can only guess. And guessing it will remain until all the pieces of this, the world's greatest jigsaw puzzle, are fitted together and the enigma of the greenhouse effect is resolved.

WINDOW 8

Wellington Worms

The dinosaurs were on the march, and so were the continents, leaving New Zealand in pole position, the closest bit of land to 90°S. No rocks laid down between 235 and 192 million years ago (the Triassic period), and indeed for a long time after, showed any sign of massive glaciation, not even those of New Zealand. The obvious conclusion is that the earth's thermal blanket was on full blast. If the heat pumps of the Carboniferous period had done their bit cooling it all down, something must have happened to warm it up again.

The very fact that the vast majority of the land masses were moving out of the grip of the polar regions was certainly enough to tip the balance. Land covered with ice and snow is a great reflector of energy; in contrast, dark rock and vegetation are good absorbers, especially of infra-red. Likewise, sea covered with ice is a good reflector, but the ice is never very thick and melts much more quickly than great masses of continental ice, giving way to the deep blue of ocean water, a much better absorber. In these modern times, troubled by the greenhouse effect, the Arctic Ocean begins to melt in summer each year, even at the North Pole, thus removing at least part of a giant solar reflector five times the size of the Mediterranean Sea.

Add to this that seeding plants growing high and dry on land quickly rot when they die. Their minerals do not go into store but are recycled to the soil, and their carbon escapes to the atmosphere as carbon dioxide. Against the background of the increasing power of the sun, more rapid recycling of carbon, and with both land and sea switching from reflecting to absorbing mode, the earth began to bask in a period of warmth. Warm and wet, for water evaporates from ice-free sea to form clouds, which water the dry earth with rain, thanks to onshore winds.

The windiest place in New Zealand is Wellington, although this may be less a fact and more a convenience of alliteration. Be that as it may, it was a trip to windy Wellington that first allowed me to peep into the next window of time.

Wellingtonians and all the capital's visitors are not only fortunate in being able to walk at will and without charge through the well-stocked Botanic Gardens, with plants drawn from all over the world; they can, at the same time, enjoy the local flora in its natural setting. Interspersed amongst the beds, borders and broadwalks are remnants of the native lowland bush that used to cover the city limits and beyond.

The father of New Zealand botany, Leonard Cockayne, wrote in 1914 that 'the Botanical Gardens of Wellington are not such in the usual acceptance of the term, for their contents are not arranged systematically or in phytogeographic or ecological groups'. Notwithstanding that, they are of peculiar interest, since no small part of their area is occupied by modified remnants of the primitive forest which filled many of the gullies and clothed many of the slopes that are now part of the city.

Moa's Ark

On my first trip to Wellington I made a pilgrimage to see just that, for it is a sad fact of modern life, and sadder still in the latter part of the century than it was in 1914, that lowland forest of almost every type has virtually disappeared from the face of the earth. I must admit that I was a bit shocked by the lack of compatible management of this unique resource and the absence of any real attempt to make use of its tremendous educational value, but my visit was almost twenty years ago. However, it was there that I came face to face, or rather cheek to cheek, with two animals I had long hoped to see.

Choosing a shady spot, well laced with tree ferns, I sat on a partly rotten log. It collapsed, setting me down in the damp litter and revealing a grey-green creeping caterpillar-like creature with a velvet coat. I had read about them, had lectures about them, and now I had almost sat on a *Peripatus*: just like the picture in the textbooks, a member of the ancient group of claw-bearers which have lived on earth for 550 million years.

An active nocturnal predator, *Peripatus* has been outdoing Spiderman for millions of nightly episodes. Raising its head, it emits two streams of slime from glands on either side of its mouth. This acts like instant glue, hardening in the air

The Wellington Botanic Gardens, an island of lowland forest in an urban sea.
LLOYD HOMER, NZ GEOLOGICAL SURVEY

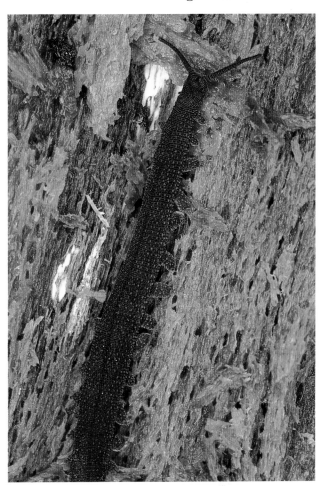

Peripatus on a rotting log.
ROD MORRIS

to produce an immensely strong thread which enmeshes its prey. I tried it by waving my little finger in a genteel afternoon-tea-type manner just in front of its feelers. Whap! Two lines immediately latched on. Once the prey is secured, the predator moves in, punctures the body wall with its jaws and sucks out the contents. Finger-licking-good! Yuk. Despite the fact that I knew my finger was in no danger, I didn't hang about. Neither did I dissect this curious beast to see if its body was divided into internal segments as the textbook says. The little pairs of stumpy legs, arranged down each side, each with a pair of tiny claws, was sufficient proof for me. So I popped it back within the mass of rotten wood and went on my way feeling elated, for I had seen one of the most famous of all the non-missing, missing links, a member of an ancient group which lies part way between the segmented worms on the one hand and the jointed-legged animals (which include crayfish, woodlice and insects) on the other.

Inspired, I started poking into cracks and crevices and scrabbling about in the deep litter that had collected in some of the gullies. It was there that I found one of the distant relatives of *Peripatus*: a native earthworm of vast proportions — well, compared with ours back home — and, what is more, it glowed in the dark.

Moa's Ark

The Maori worm can be thirty centimetres long. Mine was all of twenty-two. It burrows in the soil, eating a variety of food material, part of the energy from which it uses to produce its eerie phosphorescence. Fantastic as it is, it has a much larger cousin, the North Auckland worm, which can reach 140 centimetres in length, two in diameter, and burrow to a depth of more than three and a half metres.

These are just two of 173 sorts of native worm, which have their closest and even more gigantic relatives in Australia. Back in the Triassic period, their ancestors, along with those of *Peripatus*, were creeping and crawling their way across the warm, wet landscapes of Gondwana towards Moa's Ark, ably abetted by a gradually warming climate. Despite this, land bridges must have been in place, for earthworms can neither swim nor live in the sea. Nor were there any birds to airlift their eggs. The land must also have been clothed with vegetation to provide litter and living soil for their underground way of life.

Two hundred million years ago, what little land there was in New Zealand was covered with a fern-like plant called *Dicroidium*, which, as *Glossopteris* had been in the past, was widespread across the southern continents. So too were the ancestors of the next great group of true land plants, the cone-bearers.

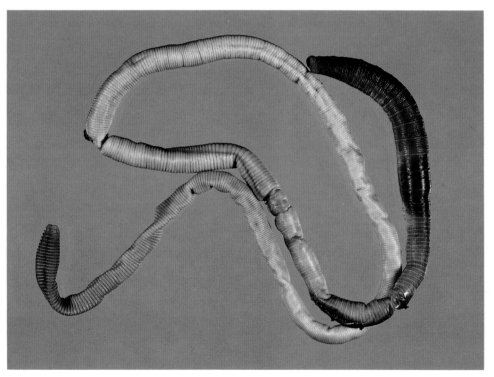

A curled-up Maori worm, *Megascolicidae*, about twenty centimetres long.
DEPARTMENT OF SCIENTIFIC AND INDUSTRIAL RESEARCH

Waipoua Giants

One hundred and fifty million years ago, New Zealand was growing fast to become a mini-continent, the bulk of which lay above 60°S. In a world still devoid of any major icecaps, it basked in a subtropical climate, and, with open land bridges to all the southern continents, plants and animals were flooding in.

According to the fossil record, the giant reptiles were late in arriving on the threshold of this new land of opportunity, and the strange mammal-like reptiles, the theropods, which had shared the world stage with the dinosaurs for at least 100 million years, never made the crossing.

The birds whose ancestry links them with the bird-hipped dinosaurs may well have arrived first. Not surprising, you will say: birds can fly across large stretches of water; no wonder they outdid their ancestors. However, among the first birds to perch on Moa's Ark were the ratites, ancestors of the moas and the kiwis, and, like them, they had lost the ability to fly. So the answer isn't that simple.

Perhaps a more fundamental question should be asked. Why do animals move? The answer is to find food and to avoid being eaten. With the continental land masses overflowing with reptiles of all shapes, sizes and dispositions, expansion of populations must have gone hand in hand with expansion of territory into pastures new and greener, which means that the plants must have got there first. Birds with the ability to fly or scramble up trees would have been part of the very first wave of colonists in new green places. Perhaps, when the flesh-eaters caught up with them, those birds that had lost the ability to fly would have been forced to move in the vanguard again. Maybe that is why they got to Moa's Ark early in the process of colonisation.

The plants that helped make all this possible were the cone-bearers. Like the seed ferns which had gone before, conifers produce pollen in 'male' cones and ovules in 'female' cones. The ovules lie naked on the cone scales, unenclosed by any protective tissue, so are very readily fertilised by wind-blown pollen. The product of this bare-faced union is a seed survival kit complete with protective coat, food store and a thin membranous wing, aerodynamically engineered for short, flutter escape.

The conifers which appear to have greened the gang plank onto Moa's Ark were relatives of the monkey-puzzles that once grew around Captain Cook's port of Whitby. Although both monkey-puzzle from Chile and the Norfolk Island pine (from where else but Norfolk Island) have been widely planted in New Zealand, the only native survivor of the once pan-global group is the kauri, and what a noble native it is!

Of all the trees in the world, *Agathis australis* has taken both the art and the craft

A dense stand of kauri rickers.

of wood-building to perfection, for, unlike the vast majority of other trees, at maturity its trunk does not taper. Its girth remains much the same from just above the roots to just below its first branches. One reason for this is its ability to cast off unwanted limbs in such a neat way that its main axis is left without external blemishes or internal knots. It has also packed its trunk with all sorts of goodies, from the gum which flows freely from wounds and helps to protect and heal, to the straightest of grains. The former protects the wood from infection; the latter gives it great flexibility, excellent strength, workability and finishing qualities. Its particularly outstanding and important attribute is that it neither shrinks nor swells when repeatedly wetted and dried. An ideal wood in every way, for turning, through furniture-making to boat- and house-building. A census of Auckland houses taken in 1861 showed that 5,236 out of 6,036 dwellings were made of kauri. A similar census of boats floating in the harbour — and, indeed, in harbours across the world — would have found this honey-coloured, low-density timber in evidence on all the best craft well into this century. It is still in great demand to this day, but fortunately or unfortunately, the supply from New Zealand has almost dried up.

The Americans are at present hosts to the world's tallest and largest trees, both contemporary records going to the fabled World Heritage redwoods, which attract millions of tourist visitors each year. However, only a hundred years ago, both records lay firmly in the South Pacific, the tallest in Australia and the largest in New Zealand.

60

Kauri cones waiting to explode.
FOREST RESEARCH INSTITUTE

Kauri bark.

Bowl turned from a subfossil kauri stump removed from a bog.

Tane Mahuta still stands, with a girth of thirteen metres all the way up to its first branches at 17.68 metres above ground level. That gives a massive trunk volume of 244.5 cubic metres at the age of 1,200 years. While we were filming this giant kauri, a party of American tourists approached along the track. Remarking on the size of the tree by which we had parked our tripod, one lady said, 'Gee, what a great tree!', then, turning the corner and seeing Tane Mahuta for the first time, she expostulated, 'Oh, my Gawd!' and stood staring at the massive trunk. It was an appropriate statement, for it is an awe-inspiring sight: a tree that has stood on that same spot since long before people arrived on the scene; a tree that has put on an incredible 0.2 cubic metres of wood throughout every average year of its life.

The modern visitor is left to imagine what it was like when great tracts of the country were covered with kauri forest, and to guess the amazement of the first people to see these trees, which are probably the largest that have ever lived. There are accounts of early explorers of the forest seeing what they took to be cliffs ahead through the trees. On closer inspection, the 'cliff' was not of rock, but of the hammer bark of yet another giant kauri.

The largest tree on official record was called Kairaru. It was measured by Percy Smith, Government Surveyor in the 1870s, at 20.12 metres in girth, 30.48 metres to the first branch, with a marketable timber volume of 808.8 cubic metres. Using the growth rate calculated for Tane Mahuta, Kairaru was at least 4,000 years of age. If only it was still alive to give up its vital statistics and to provide genetic material for all our futures! Unfortunately, it was destroyed by fire in 1886.

The kauri enigma does not stop at size, and its lifestyle is equally clouded with mystery, especially when it comes to forest regeneration. Research has indicated that natural regeneration is very rare within stands of mature trees. Low light intensity at ground level and competition with the roots of mighty parents have been cited as reasons for the failure of seedlings and saplings. There is, however, another factor of key importance, and that relates to acidification as a natural background process to life. Kauri litter, and especially kauri bark, rots very slowly, so much so that it can pile up around the trunk to a depth of more than three metres. It is also very acid and in time helps to change the nature of the soil, aiding the rain to leach many of the minerals down through the soil profile. One of the consequences of this is that the soil becomes what is known as a podsol: highly acid, devoid of most nutrients and with concrete-like layers or hard pans in the profile. The pans, which are usually rich in silica and in iron oxides, can be so hard that neither tree roots nor drainage water can penetrate the layer. Any young trees therefore will be starved of nutrients and the soil will become waterlogged, a condition shunned by kauris of any age. In a case of podsol stalemate, regeneration is impossible.

Despite the theory, in many places layer upon layer containing the remains of kauri, and especially kauri gum, are found, and often these are in areas that are today open swampland. Explanations of these conflicting phenomena are rife, but a conclusion that some sort of cyclical regeneration is taking place must surely be the answer. Earthquake shock and cyclones can and do topple the giant trees. Acting

The giant kauri Tane Mahuta.

as an enormous lever, the trunk causes the root plate to break through the hard pan, opening up a new supply of minerals, draining the soil, letting in the light and removing parental competition. In the same way, a swamp phase could lead to the death of the dominant trees and a period in which other plants could grow, eventually stablising the swamp soils and the water regime, allowing kauris to recolonise once more.

In the past, and especially in the kauri forests of Gondwana, there was another topple factor — browsing dinosaurs. For much of the early reign of the dinosaurs these vegetarians were tall and immensely large, able to browse high up into the canopy and to push at least the smaller trees over. A tree like the kauri, which can grow fast, tall and spindly in its young rikker stage, and cast off branches of its own volition, would have been well equipped when it came to living alongside the dinosaurs. And if hungry herbivores could topple the medium-sized trees, they would at least have kept the whole system stirred up and regenerating.

Regeneration would, of course, take time and need a local seed source, for although the kauri produces a cone that disintegrates while still on the tree, each individual seed, though winged, appears to move no more than 150 metres from the parent tree. So it would seem that, throughout time, the kauri forests and their ancestors were, at the best, patchworks of mature, open and regenerating stands, gradually expanding their territory wherever and whenever they could. They apparently arrived and began to take possession of the new, improving New Zealand in late Jurassic times, around 140 million years ago.

A look at the contemporary vegetation map of New Zealand shows much of the northern part of the North Island pock-marked with red dots, covering, in all, some 47,000 hectares. The legend reads 'kauri and mixed indigenous scrub', and the booklet explains that the kauri is a plant of the poorest soil, which, like the majority of the tropical rainforest soils, should have never been opened up for agriculture. History tells us that about half the area was cut over for timber and the other half was burned to make way for farming. One cannot blame the early settlers; they must have looked at the size of the trees and dreamed of the size of their crops. Abandoned to the only real crop the land can support, the cyclical succession back to kauri forest is now underway, where not hindered by the planting of exotics, or by grazing and browsing.

In an attempt to demonstrate the size of another legendary tree, called Hokianga, which had lain rotting on the forest floor for at least seventy years before it was measured, we got a lot of help from the local primary school at Waiuku. Hokianga was reputedly almost twenty-seven metres in girth, so, as a mathematics project, the pupils selected fifty-four from their school, each with an armspan of one metre. The idea was to form a double ring of five-year-olds to demonstrate the girth of the stump. I must confess it was great fun, but it wasn't too easy to accomplish, for, despite the uniformity of arm span, each was an individual and one little girl wouldn't hold hands with anyone. As the camera panned around the ring, genetic diversity, or at least its expression, was rampant — tall, short, broad, thin, blonde, brunette — you name it, the group demonstrated it. The same is, of course, true for kauri trees, each one an individual with individual characteristics waiting to be

Children from Waiuku Junior School demonstrate the size of the giant kauri Hokianga.

selected for future use. All we can do is wait and see, and bemoan the loss of genetic diversity in the past.

Until then, a walk through Waipoua or one of the other pitifully small kauri reserves allows us a glimpse through this wood-framed window into the warm past, when the full genetic potential of the ancestors of Tane Mahuta held sway across vast areas of Gondwana. Great trees, providing a home as they still do for giant worms, peripatus, ancient snails and, of course, the kiwi, New Zealand's unique flightless bird, which nests in holes in the base of the forest giants and smells out its prey from the diversity of the soil fauna, insects, slugs, snails and a host of creeping, crawling things, many of which have as yet been undiscovered by science, and are swallowed without even a Latin name.

It has been estimated that a single tree in its lifetime and in its deathtime plays host to more than 10,000 sorts of plants and animals. Each tree plays a vital role, from the moment of the union between the information contained in the pollen and the ovule until it eventually disappears from sight, once more absorbed into the soil from which it grew and to which it gives its strength. This is the cycle of kauri life, which has sustained its own place and pace of creative evolution in New Zealand for at least eighty million years. It was a tree fit to play a key role in the structure of Moa's Ark as it cast off from Gondwana and set sail across the South Pacific, leaving the Tasman Sea in its wake.

One other plant from this forest windowbox must be mentioned. *Loxsoma cunninghamii* is now a very rare fern, whose only relative is known from the fossil record of the Cretaceous period, another important member of the crew of Moa's Ark.

When, back at home, I yearn for the kauri forests of New Zealand, I go to Durham Cathedral, my university's local church. A World Heritage site and voted the most beautiful building in the world, its massive structure is supported in part by giant pillars of stone, each one like a fossil trunk of a kauri tree and each one different, like the kauri.

Within both cathedrals, the living and the people-made church of God, it is cool and shady. One is full of the songs of choristers, the other full of the songs of birds — or it was until mammals came upon the scene. The foundations of Durham Cathedral were being laid at about the same time as Moa's Ark was being colonised by the Maori.

Stephens Island

No one lives on Stephens Island any more, out there between Cook Strait and Tasman Bay. The only visitors are those who service and supply the automatic light, and the lucky few scientists and VIPs who drop in by helicopter or climb up from a boat to visit this very special sanctuary.

Partly because of its isolation and the windswept Wellington waters surrounding it, this island is one of the last strongholds of certain of the world's fauna that were members of the crew and hence once widespread across Moa's Ark. The story of the Stephens Island wren, which had its last sanctuary on this tiny scrap of land, must at this point suffice to introduce the sad tale of Moa's Ark which will develop in later chapters. Once common across New Zealand, this tiny bird was wiped out, largely because of predation by introduced mammals. It found its last nesting place on Stephens Island — that was, until the lighthouse keeper got a cat, and the wren was officially proclaimed extinct.

Thank goodness subsequent keepers have been better informed; they have taken

Stephens Island from the north.
ROD MORRIS

Hamilton's frog, *Leiopelma hamiltoni.*
ROD MORRIS

on a new role as keepers of some of the world's last remaining populations of three other animals: *Leiopelma*, the world's rarest frog; *Sphenodon*, the world's only rhynchosaur; and *Deinacrida*, the world's rarest and largest weta.

Almost at the top of the island is a pile of stones and rocks, and though it would appear to be the last place to look for an amphibian, it is indeed one of the homes of Hamilton's frog. With no pond nearby, and the whole island surrounded by the sea, you would be pardoned for exclaiming, no wonder they are so rare! But no, this is their chosen and almost their only habitat.

New Zealand has three native frogs, all are called *Leiopelma* and they are the most primitive in the world. They have probably never been very common, for, when the first was found by gold-diggers on the Coromandel, the local Maori people had no knowledge of them. As no Maori names were forthcoming, the three frogs were named Hochstetter's, Archey's and Hamilton's, in recognition of the people who made them famous.

They all have skulls with very primitive characters, and as skulls fossilise well, we know that almost identical animals were living in the late Jurassic period. Their modern descendants have no ear-drums or vocal sacs, and no webs between their toes, despite the fact that they do have vestiges of muscles which must have once wagged their tails. The latter is perhaps even more surprising when it is realised that they do not have a free-swimming tadpole stage in their life cycle. Their spawn, laid in the damp crevices of the rocks, is covered with a gelatinous capsule within which the baby froglets develop, ready to hop about and croak in a high-pitched squeak.

Sphenodon and the end of a giant weta, *Deinacrida*.
ROD MORRIS

Giant weta gets a helping hand.

Moa's Ark

Not far away from this nursery of squeaky rock-hoppers is the nesting area of an animal that, like the frogs, can be classed as a living fossil, for it has remained almost unchanged on earth for around 200 million years. If the Maori didn't know the frogs, they certainly knew and revered *Sphenodon*, giving it the name tuatara, meaning spines on the back, which it has. They also regarded it as having the wisdom of the world stored within its head — but this didn't stop tuatara from being eaten from time to time. Indeed, having lived throughout all that time, the members of its direct line of descent must have witnessed great changes as they migrated across the world to become stranded on what would be a cooling Moa's Ark. Fortunately for the tuatara, whereas most reptiles like to get out and about between 25 and 38°C, its ancient form and cold blood function well between 12 and 17°. As reptiles go, the tuatara is a real cool customer, a fact that must have ensured its survival during the subsequent voyage of Moa's Ark.

Perhaps the most unusual feature of this unique animal is the presence, when young, of the vestiges of a third, centrally placed eye: an eye that, having sampled the information of 200 million years of life, took on a new role as a gland, the pineal, which helps control the bodily functions in more advanced animals. A synthesis of the wisdom of the world in its head? But that would be pushing myth too far, just as the introduction of dogs and rats pushed the tuatara to the edge of extinction, first on the mainland and then on the other offshore islands: one reason why few people are allowed to land and gaze upon the singular beast. However, should you be in Invercargill (and do make it in the oyster season), a visit to the local museum will let you see live tuatara, complete with pineal eye, in where else but a tuatarium. Safe within its confines, they are breeding in captivity, with every zoo round the world waiting like expectant godmothers.

The third animal in the natural selection collection of Stephens Island is the giant weta. These giants — and they are giant, some weighing nearly seventy grams — are flightless crickets. If their rat-like size and droppings aren't enough to put you off, then their array of sickle-shaped spikes and their ferocious-looking jaws will. There is, however, no need to worry: they can scratch but don't bite, for they feed in the litter on the forest floor. Once widespread across the mainland, they too have found their penultimate resting places on rat-free islands, for rats relish wetas, perhaps getting their own back on the insect clan for the fleas that plague them. Again, the lineage of these great insects stretches back across almost 200 million years, with its foundation in Queensland and others parts of the southern land masses.

The photograph I tried to get for my collection was the reflection of a weta in a tuatara's eye. As both appeared to be living in close proximity, I crawled on hands and knees until I found the place: a tuatara sitting stock-still like a setter, signalling the position of its prey. I crept in, macro at the ready, closer and closer. Click! I got a photo of thin air and the setter got the better of the weta. To cap the story, as I was crawling back, still thinking I had the picture of a lifetime, I got bitten, or at least my finger did, by a medium-sized tuatara. No wonder they call them beak head!

Whirinaki Podocarps

For a long time it was thought that the dinosaurs never made it across the gangplank before Moa's Ark began to draw away from port about eighty million years ago. No fossil remains of the tyrant lizards were found, and questions were asked regarding the continuity of the bridges that linked the parts of Gondwana and the speed of dispersion of those lumbering leviathans of the land. It was, of course, pointed out that not all dinosaurs were built on the grand scale: many were small in size, even when compared to the flightless birds that appear to have beaten them onto the Ark.

The seas around the Ark overflowed with marine reptiles, and battles of dino-saurian dimensions took place in what is now North Canterbury, for there are abundant fossils to prove it. On land it was a case of no such luck until the mid-1980s, when an amateur geologist by the name of Joan Wiffen found the proof everyone was hoping for. While fossicking in a tributary of the Te Hoe River in the Hawke's Bay area, she found a bone that, though no more than five centimetres long, was shown to be part of the tail of a medium-sized (seven metres long or thereabouts), flesh-eating theropod dinosaur. The bone was preserved in marine sediments, suggesting that the animal itself may have made a living fossicking along the shore, eating nice juicy things like stranded ammonites and belemnites, both of which are related to modern-day squids and octopi, which are themselves related to snails.

Not long after this exciting discovery, Joan Wiffen found another bone, part of the pelvis of a vegetarian bird-hipped dinosaur (splendidly named a hypsilophodont), which must have lived at least in the margin of the forest. The strangest thing is that they are both from about the same period, sixty-five to seventy million years ago, long after Moa's Ark had severed all intercontinental connections and was sailing dangerously close to the South Pole. Not a very nice spot for an animal, whether cold- or warm-blooded.

Fossil fossickers, amateur and professional, the search is on! For there must be other skeletons under the hatches of Moa's Ark, proof of the local stamp of the dinosaurs, even if they did make a pier-head jump into the safety of the Ark. Whatever new evidence comes to light, one thing is certain: we will never find a living dinosaur, for they all went to the wall of extinction not long after those two bones were swept out to sea and into the natural history books.

The dinosaurs may have come and gone, and with them most of the forests which paved and powered the way for their 163-million-year era of success. But the descendants of the trees that provided them with a home, and perhaps a barrier that slowed down their rate of advance, can still be seen, and nowhere better than through another timber-framed window, called Whirinaki, not far from Rotorua.

Caroline Houston of the New Zealand Geological Survey with a fossil mosasaur skull.
The mosasaur, a gigantic marine reptile with flippers and a strong jaw, lived eighty
million years ago.
NZ GEOLOGICAL SURVEY, DSIR

The podocarps are a group of conifers whose seed bears a fleshy appendage, a
lump called a foot. Despite the fact that it isn't a fruit in the true sense of the word
— fruits are only produced by flowering plants — the 'foot' is full of nutrients and
energy, and so attracts birds to feed. The seed, being much less digestible than the
foot, passes through the bird to be planted out, each in its own supply of slow-release
organic fertiliser, somewhere else in the forest. It is in this way that the seeds of
kahikatea, totara, rimu, matai and miro, the contemporary forest giants, were dis-
persed throughout New Zealand. Like them, the army of their ancestors footslogged
its way across New Zealand, marching in the stomachs of flying and running
messengers, arriving on the local scene while the gangplanks were still in position.

Like the kauri, the ancestors of the podocarps were well able to stand up to the
attention of the dinosaur mob. They grew rapidly in height, producing unpalatable
foliage on a stout trunk, supported by buttress roots, especially when growing in wet
places, and in their mature years were un-topplable by winds and dinosaurs alike.

The browsing dinosaurs were by this time being scaled down, perhaps in part
by selection. Those that were able to nip off amongst the tree trunks, where the large
carnivores couldn't follow without enormous expenditure of energy, would certainly
have been at an advantage. The plants, too, were changing their strategies of

survival, and sometime and at some place in the world the first flower-bearing plant must have unleashed a whole new armamentarium of chemical warfare. Flowering plants produce pollen grains in special sacs called anthers. These may be carried by insects, birds, mammals, wind or water to the egg inside the ovule. The nuptial pathway is complex, with all sorts of obstacles en route. For a start, the ovules are not vulnerable, lying ready on a cone scale, but are enclosed in an ovary. The way into this is directed through solid tissue called a style, which, unlike the stiles of the countryside, is there to impede, not to speed, access. The pollen grains are received on a landing pad called the stigma. The signs on this chemically adhesive doormat are both of welcome and rejection. Within the style are chemicals that speed or impede the growth of a visiting pollen tube, thus in part selecting the successful mate. The pollen tube must grow down from the pollen grain through the tissue of the style to deposit the genetic message contained within the male cells and so trigger a complex union. The result of this union, hidden deep within the tissues of the flower, is a seed enclosed in a fruit; a seed kitted out with a foodstore only when the union is complete. Nothing goes to waste.

Exactly where the first flower opened we do not know, but much evidence points to the area of Gondwana that is now Australia. Within the contemporary flora of Australia there are more than 592 species of flowering plants, all of which have retained very primitive structural characteristics. Most of them have their homes in the rapidly diminishing tropical rainforests of Queensland. Only one need be mentioned, its name *Austrobaileya scandens*, its pollen grains closely resembling the oldest-known pollen grains of flower-bearing plants: pollen that was blowing around on earth 100 million years ago during the birth-time of the flowers and the demise of the dinosaurs.

At that time, the table manners of many of the herbivorous reptiles were changing. The large, long-necked and 'stand up on your back legs and reach for the canopy' browsers were being superseded by smaller, big-beaked forms which fed closer to the ground. The ferns and seed ferns, which still abounded on the forest floor, and the seedlings of conifers, including podocarps, were all under attack, and so the way was opened up for a new group of plants with new attributes of survival: rapid growth in the seedling stage, with leaves and shoots which could be nipped off and would sprout and grow again; plants with small, light seeds which could be blown upwards and then grow, perching in the high branches out of harm's way; plants with strategies of early reproduction, producing fruits which would carry the seeds to new areas opened up when stripped of their vegetation by the parrot-bill dinosaurs; plants containing new chemicals the like of which made them distasteful and poisonous to the new brigade of low-down browsers. Whether these new armour-plated ground-level mowers suffered from hay fever we may never know. We do know, both from the microfossils like pollen grains, and the macrofossils like stems, roots, flowers and fruits and, of course, the bones and armour-plating, that from this stage on the dinosaurs were doomed to extinction. As they disappeared, species by species, genus by genus, family by family, the flower-bearers took over from the podocarps the role as the major provenders and as important structural components of Moa's Ark, and indeed the post-dinosaur world.

Seed and fleshy aril of kahikatea, *Dacrycarpus dacrydioides*.

Male cones of matai, *Prumnopitys taxifolia*.

Flowers of the rewarewa, *Knightia excelsa*.

Whirinaki giant totara, *Podocarpus totara*.

As you walk through Whirinaki, the last five per cent of the dense, tall-stemmed podocarp forest left in the world, cast your eyes like the long-extinct dinosaur browsers, down on the lower canopy. Gaze, not graze, upon the seedlings and saplings of rewarewa. Rather like its neighbouring podocarps, everything about rewarewa is tall and thin: a narrow, tapering tree up to thirty metres tall; long, thin, pale leaves in lax bunches when young, but stiff and upright in maturity. Long, thin, red buds open to reveal curling petals and eventually long, thin, rust-coloured fruits. Rewarewa is a member of a very primitive family of flower-bearers called the Proteaceae, a family still doing well in Australia and South Africa, as they have since dinosaur times.

There are many theories concerning the extinction of the dinosaurs and a range of other living things, both on land and in the seas, at the end of the Cretaceous period, sixty-five million years ago. They range from the 'big bang' theory of a meteorite falling on the earth, to the 'constipation' theory, which must have stopped many other large objects falling on the earth. The first suggests the immense impact of an extraterrestrial body sufficient to affect the whole globe, spreading iridium-rich debris (which is certainly in evidence for the right period) and bringing death and destruction to many plants and animals. The latter theory suggests that if large animals were forced to eat up not only their vegetables but all the flowers, fruits and the new chemicals they contained, they may well have become terminally constipated.

Whatever the reason, the ruling reptiles disappeared, to be replaced by the up-and-coming mammals; the seed ferns also became extinct, and the true ferns and the conifers began to move into second place, living it up down in the shade of the flower-bearing trees. The mammals, in the guise of the pouch-bearing marsupials and the egg-laying monotremes, made it as far as Australia and took over the potential of that island continent. They are still there, doing well, mainly because very few of the other, main line of warm-blooded ascent, the true mammals, ever got that far.

Moa's Ark broke away before the jet-set true mammals arrived on the east coast of Gondwana and set sail with a motley crew, mariners of the ancient past and midshipmen of future lines of ascent. From this point on, any new members of the ship's company were going to have to fly or use some other means of trans-Tasman or trans-Pacific passage.

Te Anau Beech

Ry the end of the dinosaur times, around sixty-five million years ago, Gondwana
was really cracking up. India and Africa had gone their separate ways north,
and Moa's Ark was doing the same, with Antarctica sliding across the South Pole,
still linked with Australia and, to a lesser extent, South America. Warm-blooded,
furry, milk-producing mammals with pouches were widespread across Australia and
Antarctica; some were in South America, but none got to New Zealand. Over the rest
of the world they were being rapidly replaced by the true, or placental, mammals,
the offspring of which complete much more of their development within the uteri
of their mothers, a much safer set-up than a post-natal pouch — a womb with
a view.

Although a large land mass was moving across the Pole, there are still no signs
of glaciation in the rocks laid down at this time. Quite the contrary, for the Antarctic
provides many fossils, thus proving the presence of dense forests of southern beech
and pointing to a cold-temperate or even cool-temperate climate in the ultra-
Antipodes. Well-marked annual rings in the fossil wood prove that the climate was
of a seasonal nature, seasons of plenty and seasons of hardship.

Despite the lack of any ice sheet, the flagship mini-continent of Moa's Ark was
being worn away by massive erosion, its mighty mountains being reduced to flat
peneplains, encroached upon and, in places, inundated by the sea. No ice, lots of
shallow water and land vegetation meant the planet was in heat-absorption mode,
and most of the world's water was in free-liquid form; sea levels were high, rainfall
was heavy and water erosion rife.

Erosion carried enormous amounts of ground rock downhill to be deposited in
deltas, creating new lowlands and shallowing the water over continental shelves.
Lowland swamps, made up of a mixture of wetland forests and more open vegetation, began to lay down new deposits of coal, trapping carbon dioxide once more
into long-term storage.

Our chosen windows onto the late Cretaceous world are two, both in the south-
west of the South Island. The one straddles the mouth of the Haast River, where
ridge upon ridge of sand dunes mirror the interplay between sea, wind, rain and
coastal flatlands. The dune ridges are covered with forest, a mixture of plants from
dinosaur and post-dinosaur times, dominated by podocarps and beeches, the
shallows between supporting open water and swamp in which peat, the forerunner
of coal, is being laid down to this day. It is without doubt one of the most perfect
natural-forested dune systems left in the world, as yet little studied and fortunately
untouched by the developments that have wrecked much of the adjacent coastal
plains, which were, in the not-too-distant past, covered with similar forest.

76

Mosquito Hill mirrored in a pool of the Haast River, South Westland.

In an area now plagued by unemployment, thanks to the demise of uneconomic industries like coal mining and logging, a new direction of enterprise is urgently needed. Logging has already ruined millions of hectares of land, for, like the kaurilands of the north, the forest soils of the wet south-west cannot support viable farming: with the trees go many of the minerals, including the base chemicals, such as lime, which help to keep acidity at bay. The timber industry also went much too far in the direction of the mountains, removing the living skin which held the soil on steep, rain-washed slopes, speeding erosion and inundation of what good farm-land there was along the river valleys.

The whole area is of World Heritage class, and once its international status has been ratified, the new enterprise which will rejuvenate the economy of the area must centre on tourism. A visitor and interpretation centre at Haast is a must, with board-walks enabling locals and visitors alike to step back in time and meet their future in their past, their links with Gondwana.

If oak is the heartwood of England, then *Nothofagus*, the southern beech, which is a member of the same family of flowering plants, performed the same function for most of Gondwana. Back in those far-off days there were many more types of beech on Moa's Ark, including some of the warmth-demanding species still found today in other parts of the Southern Hemisphere. Contemporary New Zealand boasts four species, red, hard, black and silver — the mountain beech is only a form of black beech, which along with silver, does well in the uplands. All are evergreen and all are endemic, which means they grow naturally only in New Zealand. They do have close relatives in other far-flung parts of the world — New Caledonia, eastern Australia, Tasmania and South America — and they are often planted as ornamentals in gardens, even in the far north of the Northern Hemisphere.

The true southern beech forests of Moa's Ark and of Tierra Del Fuego and other parts of South America are very similar to look at and have many strange and beautiful things in common.

Mosses, liverworts and lichens abound in both areas. One lichen genus called *Sticta* has over seventy species, mostly growing on the bark of beeches in New Zealand, while many of the other 330 members are found doing the same thing in South America. Another lichen with many species across on the other side of the Pacific is *Menegazzia*, a member of a genus which makes large patches, twenty centimetres in diameter, on the trunks of South Island beeches. Not only are there lichens, the forests of both areas provide a home for a parasitic fungus called *Cyttaria gunnii*, which produces its orange, strawberry-like fruiting bodies on branches and twigs. They are eaten by local people and birds alike in both areas, although I must confess they taste a little insipid to a passing botanist. Please be careful; if you do decide to dabble in mycophagy (that is, eating toadstools and other fungi), sarcophagy could be just around the corner: some are very poisonous. Become a

Fruiting bodies of the golfball fungus, *Cyttaria*, on silver beech.

Silver beech, Cascade River
GUY SALMON

Wet interior of a beech forest in North Westland.

Mountain beech forest in the Waimakariri Valley, Canterbury.

Interior of mountain beech forest.

good taxonomist, someone who can identify living things, not a dead dinosaur. There are also some very primitive sap-sucking bugs which live in the moss mats of both regions, attacking the roots of the beeches.

All these and many more pieces form part of the unique jigsaw that fits the countries and the continents back together and shows us how the beeches were able to take over the earth, along with the other flower-bearing plants. Beech fruit, or mast, as it is called in many places, has poor years, when little or no fruit is produced, and mast years, in which the forest floor overflows with the crop. Birds pay them but little attention, and, although some of the fruit have a small wing, it is woody and so does not fly far. Carried along in streams and rivers, their ultimate destination must be the sea, in which they cannot survive, and so the beech mast is left stranded on the beaches, proof positive that at one time the land masses of Gondwana were in close enough contact for the beeches to expand their territories in their own slow way.

Moa's Ark got its beeches, its orange fungal golf balls and its sap-sucking bugs, but it didn't get any land mammals to live within its beech forests or on its beaches. A fact that our second window on the late Cretaceous world proves beyond doubt.

The Haast region awaits proper tourist development which will allow the world to marvel at its perfection. Lake Te Anau, one of the most beautiful lake locations in the world, has already been opened up to the tourist trade. One of the best ways to take in its beech-clad mountains and beech-fringed beaches is by boat. The recycled steamer *Quintin McKinnon*, which takes the tramping mob off to the start of the Milford Track, is ideal, for even on the rainiest of days you can view the panoply of forest from the comfort of its saloon, complete with a cup of tea.

The old boat came in very handy when we were filming this particular section of the television series, for our own ultra-modern, high-speed outboard craft broke down, leaving us stranded afloat in a landlocked sea. Fortunately for us, the steamer appeared over the horizon and took us in tow.

The subject of that part of the series was the deer exclosures which have been erected near the shore of the lake to ascertain the effects of browsing by deer, first introduced into the area in the 1950s. An exclosure is designed to keep animals out, but as you approach it through the overbrowsed forest, it looks as if it has been put there to keep the plants in. Outside the netted fences there is little in the way of lush undergrowth or tree seedlings and saplings. Inside each fence, the forest floor is alive with new growth, new generations of forest plants.

The deer appear to take all things green, lush and juicy, including such primitive flower-bearers as rewarewa, emphasising the fact that it was not just what Moa's Ark took on board that was of importance — of equal and critical importance was what got left behind on the beaches.

The Voyage
of the Ark

Bats on Little Barrier

Moa's Ark continued its passage north into warm temperate waters and began to enjoy a climate much as it is today, in isolation. New sea floor stopped forming in the Tasman about sixty million years ago and left it with a gap of 1,850 kilometres, three hours as the jumbo jet flies to or from Australia. A long hop, but quite late in this phase of sea-floor expansion certain early aviators must have made the crossing.

One of these was a mammal, a member of the insect-eating Chiroptera, or bat family. The others were the ancestors of three groups of birds — the wrens, the thrushes and the wattlebirds. No need to crow about that, you might say, but be patient, wait and see.

Antarctica was still partly covered with beech forest, and coal-forming swamps were doing their bit to remove carbon dioxide from greenhouse circulation, so Antarctica was still open for a flying visit. However, the main immigration route was most probably from South-East Asia via Papua New Guinea and Australia. Island-hopping and storm-driven, with many stopovers on the way, they came, they soared and they conquered in a land where there were no nasty, flesh-eating, egg-sucking, fruit- and nectar-stealing mammals to compete with. Moa's Ark became an avian paradise as birds began to make use of all its riches and fill all the niches within mountains, grasslands, forest, swamps, coasts and inshore waters alike.

Modern New Zealand has only two native land mammals — warm-blooded, milk-producing animals that got there of their own accord. Both are bats.

Primaeval bats probably developed from a small, tree-living, shrew-like creature which, once it had gained wings through modification of its five-fingered forearm, spread rapidly through the warmer parts of the world, places where there were lots of insects all the year round. Sleeping hanging upside down presents all sorts of problems, but hibernation is a real headache.

The short-tailed bat is an old-timer on Moa's Ark, and complex tests have shown its nearest relatives to be in South America; it is a member of an ancient group, very low down the batting order. Its ancestors must have flown and been blown from land mass to land mass until they found a safe home where they could spread their wings and stretch their legs. One of this bat's primitive characteristics is that it is very active and at home down on the ground, where it scuttles about, crawling up trees and flitting amongst the trunks and branches.

About the same time, and following much the same route, members of the three families of birds also spied Moa's Ark. Though related to the wrens, thrushes and crows, all three should bear the label New Zealand in front of their names, for they are today found nowhere else in the world. They are all members of the great group

A lesser short-tailed bat, *Mystacina tuberculata*.
MIKE DANIEL, DSIR

A kokako, *Callaeas cinerea*, acting suspiciously.
ROD MORRIS

Flowers of the forest shrub taurepo,
Rhabdothamnus solandri.

Rifleman, *Acanthisitta chloris*, at nest.
ROD MORRIS

of perching birds, or passerines, the weight of whose bodies make their toes grip round branches and twigs — a group that makes up more than sixty per cent of all the world's contemporary birds, showing just how tight they can sit.

The New Zealand wrens are all small insect-eaters and may have evolved before Gondwana split up. There are, or rather were, four species: the rifleman, once wide-spread, but now uncommon and endangered over some of its range; the rock wren, which we shall meet later in the alpine zones of the South Island; the bush wren, another South Islander, once common but now thought to be extinct; and the Stephens Island wren, which used to be widespread on the mainland but is now definitely extinct.

The New Zealand wattlebirds are distantly related to the crows and may well have been on Moa's Ark before it set sail. Three species once sang their hearts out, to the delight of the ship's company: but the fabled huia is now extinct. The saddle-back is no longer present on the mainland, and the kokako is declining in the North Island and is very rare, or extinct, in the South. Piopio, the New Zealand thrush, was, or still is, a bird of the forest floor, though it is probably now extinct. Many specimens of all these birds stuff the museums and zoology departments of the world, for they have all gone into major decline over the past 150 years. The reasons for this sad state of affairs are destruction of habitat and the introduction of competitors and predators, the worst of which are, without doubt, all mammals. It seems almost impossible that the ancestors of these and so many other unique plants and animals rode the stormy seas of environmental change for at least sixty million years in the safety of Moa's Ark, only to be wiped out by humans, the sole animal that can have any understanding of what they are doing.

In order to step back into this song-filled time frame, we are now forced to take to the high seas and head out for an offshore island where precautions have been taken to prepare a lifeboat ready, not only for our landing but for the safety of these ancient winged and many flightless mariners of Moa's Ark.

Little Barrier Island is New Zealand's most outstanding wildlife sanctuary, where, thanks to a phenomenal amount of work by dedicated people, many now-rare animals and plants are riding out the tides of death and destruction that are still washing over the mainland.

So precious is its cargo that landing on the island is forbidden by law. Visits can only be made if you come complete with written permission from the Hauraki Gulf Maritime Park Board, Department of Conservation, 60 Cook Street, Auckland. It's well worth the effort and the wait, for there is a long waiting list. If you want to visit paradise, a paradise of colour, movement and song, a paradise every New Zealander could experience in their own back yard if only their forebears had been a little more careful, it's worth going to a lot of trouble.

To see the ancient bats, you must be there in the evening: they spend the day asleep in hollow trunks of totara or rimu, as they probably have for sixty million years, so please do not disturb. They share their hollow trunks with bell-birds, not for resting but for feeding, especially when they have young in the nest. Despite the fact that they are nectar-feeders, bellbirds visit the hollow and rotten trunks to collect grubs, insects and spiders: high-protein tucker to feed fledgling campanologists. Pairing between bellbirds begins in late autumn, and then their perfect pitch of bells rings out for all to hear. Mating time is best, but at any time of year the chimes are there, tuned to perfection, the season's harmonious tin-tinnabulation. How the bats sleep in their belltrees — well, belfry isn't quite the right word — is anybody's guess. And we can only surmise how many bellbirds rang in the new year of 1769 and how many joined the chorus of tui, huia, saddlebacks and kokako which piped James Cook aboard Moa's Ark.

The short-tailed bat also rests (they don't nest, for like all true mammals, they bear live young) in caves and beneath the flaking bark of trees. The flaking treebark also shelters another now very rare animal, *Deinacrida*, the giant weta: a member of the ancient order of flightless crickets. A rare combination indeed, and one that you might think would lead to a new record of extinction. An insect sleeping with an insect-eater? But the boot would appear to be on the other foot, for the weta is the heaviest insect in the world and can weigh in at almost seventy grams, the bat weighs only a few grams. Fortunately for the *Red Data Book*, which lists rare and endangered species, these rat-sized insects are vegetarians and feed on rotting wood, leaves and the like, and so the bats are safe. Once widespread on the northern main-land, they are now almost confined to island sanctuaries. Like the saddlebacks and the kokako, the wetas have been re-introduced to Little Barrier Island in the last desperate bid for their survival. They were introduced only after all the feral cats — domestic cats that had run wild — had been removed. There are millions of domestic cats in the world, each with a good caring home and each giving great pleasure to its owner, like you; unfortunately, there are many more feral cats trying to eke out an existence. All the scientists did was to end their struggle and allow our unique fauna to have a chance to survive.

Of the wrens, the rifleman is the most difficult of the Little Barrier birds to see, and its *zzitt* is so high-pitched that it is difficult for some people to hear. The name comes from the olive-green plumage of the male adult, which is the same colour as the coats worn by the members of a New Zealand military unit.

If you see a thrush on the island, it will be an introduced European, for all the New Zealand thrushes are extinct, although some question that conclusion and search on. If they are eventually found alive and well, they will probably be removed to Little Barrier Island or some other well-prepared lifeboat island, where, surrounded by a barrier of water, they may survive into the next century and beyond.

There is so much more to see on Little Barrier, and I have already stepped out of my time frame by including the bellbirds and the tui, but you can't go to this sanctuary without hearing from them. However, before climbing on the boat and stepping back into the real problems of the twentieth century, it is well worth looking for one of the strangest insects on earth — so strange that in 1775 it was the first insect ever to be described from New Zealand.

The giant giraffe beetle, *Lasiorhynchus barbicornis* is seventy-five millimetres long to the tip of its very long snout, which has two feelers and remote-controlled teeth. The female has this unique type of teeth, but her antennae are positioned

Pohutukawa forest on Little Barrier Island.

halfway down the snout, where they don't get in the way when she bores deep holes in wood in which to lay her eggs. This extraordinary creature, a member of a very primitive group of weevils, was once quite common on the mainland, where today it is almost as rare as remote-controlled teeth.

We were privileged to spend a day filming on the island as guests of the Department of Conservation, and Ranger Alex Dobbins and his wife, Mike. They live in paradise and they know it, but are willing to share its secrets with all who really care.

Alex Dobbins and *Nestor meridionalis*, a friendly kaka.

Riccarton Bush

The Tasman Sea completed its period of expansion as the local area of sea-floor spreading shifted south-east and began to ease Australia and Antarctica apart. One was pushed north and the other massive bulk was sent swinging south.

Moa's Ark itself was still under massive attack from the elements: though in part the Ark was warm and even subtropical, erosion was rife. The bush vegetation must have done its best to hold the protective soil in place, but it was no match for millions of years of heavy rainfall, and I mean *heavy*. In an average year, every square metre of the wettest parts of Fiordland is subjected to the impact of 10 tonnes of water. As the mountains were inexorably ground down and their remains swept into the sea, forests of all types were destroyed, inundated and regenerated, a continuous process of change that kept the whole place well stirred and both extinction and creative replacement on the go.

The already-extensive swamps in Northland, Waikato, Southland and along the coast of the South Island extended their soggy anaerobic grip on the worn-down landscapes, and the peat so formed was later covered with sediments, compressed and turned into coal. A by-product of this new Eocene age coal may well have been the oil and natural gas now being harvested from beneath the seabed around Taranaki. The mind boggles to think what would have happened if Taranaki's volcanic vent had disgorged its molten magma via the oil- and gas-bearing reservoirs. At a guess, there would have been an instant release of greenhouse gas overshadowed by a huge pall of smoke. But, of course, combustion requires oxygen, and could the air have got in quick enough to fuel the flame? Who knows, let the mind boggle on.

Although nothing like as large in capacity as the coal pumps of the Carboniferous, those of the Paleocene and Eocene must have moved a lot of carbon into store, and perhaps it was this that helped tip the balance towards cooler times.

Antarctica was being affected by ice, at least on its mountain tops, fifty million years ago. Over the next ten million years, the small ice caps expanded to form ribbon-like glaciers, which eventually reached the sea, calving icebergs that must have become features of the ocean currents circling around the cooling continent. It was to take another twenty-five million years of cooling to bring the whole of Antarctica under ice, hitting the refrigeration button which led to the whole series of modern glaciations and to the extinction of so many of the world's living things.

A trip south from Auckland across the rich farming country of Waikato, or further south across the Manawatu, Wairarapa, Taranaki or the Canterbury Plains, gives some idea of the flatness of the worn-down hulk of Moa's Ark. Almost to prove it, much of these areas were peat-forming swampland before extensive drainage opened them up to the plough and the cow over the past 150 years.

Without doubt, the most accessible windows onto this particular time slot of our story are in surburban Christchurch. The first is Riccarton Bush, a haven of swamp forest which, thanks to the foresight of the local Maori and of the Deans family among the original Pakeha settlers of the area, and their descendants, is still in its natural state. Well, as natural as it can be with concrete access track, blocked drains and piped irrigation water. Its most outstanding features are tall, straight kahikatea, each with their textbook plank-buttress roots snaking across the soggy ground for many metres in every direction. These roots give ample support to the towering trunks and dive down to tap underground aquifers. If you follow the tracks, and please don't deviate from the wandering and narrow (for too many feet off the path will kill these roots and, in effect, love the place to death), you can spend a happy, wholesome, wilderness hour or more, not a stone's throw from elegant back gardens.

On your way back to civilisation, take in the latest exhibition or poetry reading at Riccarton House. Then, as you step, ride or drive back through the suburbs — complete with chipboard, fake and real brick, kauri and pine weatherboarding, fine Anglican churches, schools and shops — stop and ponder on this fact. In 1844, one Frederick Tuckett, who had been sent to find a site for the Free Church of Scotland, lost his way in the swamps, which then extended for four times the area of Lake Ellesmere, and spent the night soaking wet.

Kahikatea in Riccarton Bush, Christchurch.

An aerial view of Travis Swamp, Christchurch.
KELVIN NICHOLL, LINCOLN COLLEGE

The last remnant of this great and dismal swamp can still be seen a few kilometres from Riccarton, though while I'm writing this I have my fingers crossed, for Travis Swamp is under threat from developers. The pleas of the protectors are many, for the last tiny area of swamp has twenty-nine species of native birds and forty-four native plants, with five recognisable plant associations, all rare in the Christchurch area. One part of the submission on birds must suffice:

'Travis Swamp supports the third largest population of pukeko (c. 300) in Canterbury. The other two major habitats for pukeko are Lake Ellesmere (300–500) and the Christchurch Drainage Board's sewage treatment works (600). There has been a sharp decline in pukeko at Lake Ellesmere from 2,000–3,000 in 1965 to 300–500 in 1982.'

One is forced to ask whether the future generations of Christchurch who want to see New Zealand's commonest and most striking birds should be forced either to travel miles into the country or visit paddocks around their own sewage treatment plant? A dismal prospect for birds and humans alike.

It was probably the tales of the dismal swampland around what is now Canterbury, carried back by William Tuckett and his companion Dr Munro, 'who could not comprehend how a causeway could be built between Port Cooper and a settlement on the promising plains', that led to the establishment of Dunedin as Scotland's main spearhead into the riches of New Zealand. Not to miss out, we too will travel to Dunedin to open the next porthole onto the epic voyage of Moa's Ark.

With cooler waters now able to circulate around the separating continent of Antarctica and Australia, one of the most important features of the southern oceans must have been created. The Antarctic Convergence is no imaginary line of mathematical

93

convenience dividing up the face of the world, like the Equator, but is a living thing, a tenuous, ever-shifting belt of mixing water. It is a zone of upwelling where cold, dense, south polar water meets the warmer water of temperate latitudes; a zone of mineral enrichment that feeds the myriad of miniature floating plants which are themselves the basis for the food chains of the sea and help provide the world with much of its oxygen.

It was into these warm-cool waters, further enriched by erosion from the land, that creative evolution launched a whole race of new companions for Moa's Ark: another group of flightless birds, which feed at sea and, in the absence of a floating egg or nest — things not yet achieved by avian evolution — return to land to court, mate, incubate and raise their chicks. Their homes were lands like New Zealand, South America, Antarctica and the south of Africa and Australia, much of the coasts of which were covered with forest forty million years ago.

These birds are the penguins, and today there are no fewer than sixteen species and nine subspecies which spread their flipper-like wings to help them keep warm or cold around the coasts of all those countries and many offshore islands. Moa's Ark still counts no fewer than seven species — about a third of the world's total — as members of her ship's company.

Along the coast near Dunedin, which was for a long time the commercial capital of New Zealand, *Megadyptes*, the last-remaining member of the most ancient order of the penguins, may still be found. The yellow-eyed penguin — hoiho (noise-shouter) as the Maori people call it — is the third-largest and the rarest and most endangered penguin in the world.

Unlike all other penguins, which come ashore only during the breeding season, the hoiho heaves itself ashore every day of the year; yes, even bank holidays and Sundays, so if you live in Dunedin you can pop down and see them any evening. In mid-August, partnerships are formed and nest sites selected; these then become home base to which they return every night. Between mid-September and mid-October, two greenish-white eggs are laid and incubated for some forty-three days. Both parents share the incubation and the six weeks' baby-sitting, one parent staying in the nest while the other parent swims off to fish in the deep waters not far off-shore. When the provider returns in the late afternoon, a wonderful pre-feeding duet of trills and cries takes place before tea-time gets underway. The meal is always the same, part-digested fish and squid. By the end of the six weeks, the chicks are so big and so demanding that both parents must go to the offshore supermarket each day to fish. The daily chore then continues until late February or March, when the chicks, complete with waterproof no-fluff plumage, waddle off to sea on a 500-kilometre trip to feeding grounds in the north. A trip from which fewer than thirty per cent ever return, and only fifteen per cent ever survive to breed.

The exhausted parents stay put, having only a few weeks to prepare for the hazards of a four-week moult, during which they can't go to sea to feed. At this time it is absolutely crucial that they have a safe, secluded, sheltered site where they can rest in peace, ready to start the whole cycle once more.

All this may be seen on the coasts close to the clamour of Dunedin — but for how much longer? The problem is that, for millions of years, the ancestors of the hoiho

Hoiho, the yellow-eyed penguin,
Megadyptes antipodes.
ROD MORRIS

Yellow-eyed penguin country,
Double Bay, Otago Peninsula.

have come ashore to nest in the safety of forest devoid of any predators. Today, there is little or no coastal forest left, and a lot of introduced predators for them and their chicks to contend with, including humans with motorcycles, cats and ferrets.

If the hoiho was a communal breeder, like most of the other penguins, perhaps the ferrets would not be too much of a worry, because there would always be plenty of adults about to fend off the intruders. Unfortunately, being birds of the forest, they are very private things and will not mate or rear their chicks out in the open where other penguins and passers-by can see. So breeding sites have become rarer and rarer as cattle, sheep and rabbits graze all the cover down to ground level. Where there is sufficient cover of the right sort, the cats and ferrets take their toll of the chicks during the first five critical weeks. Yellow-eyed penguins never developed anti-predator behaviour. Cats and ferrets become so bold that they kill penguin chicks even though their parents are still brooding them — and dogs kill the adults. Poor hoiho doesn't know how to deal with the situation at all. I think one of the saddest things I have seen were nine parents struggling their way up the steep cliffs — no easy matter for a bird so perfectly adapted to life at sea — only to stand guard beside the flax plants which hide their nests, nests that had been robbed by ferrets. Each day they returned to keep their lonely vigil until a new breeding season started. The Yellow-Eyed Penguin Trust has been set up to slow and reverse this trend towards extinction, and the whole world holds its breath and waits.

Before we leave this very sad window on the past, speculate on the fact that during the early evolution of the penguins, the vast majority of these southern coasts were covered with forest and bush. The communal behaviour of many of the developing penguin lines may well have been forced on them by predation, and by the fact that one of their ancestral land masses was slowly but surely becoming deforested and covered with ice.

Taiaroa Royal Nursery

We will stay in the environs of Dunedin as we pass through the next time window into the Oligocene period. What is more, we are going to get an aerial overview of royal dimensions, thanks to another bird that shares this stretch of coast with the hoiho.

Twenty-five million years ago, the southern continents were being prised apart, almost as if they shunned contact with the dying continent of Antarctica, which was stuck across the Pole. The last link to be broken was a wedge of shallow water between Tasmania and Antarctica's Victoria Land. Ice was forming on the central mountains of Antarctica, its weight depressing the continent and its glaciers eroding the river valleys and spilling minerals and icebergs into the sea, where it slowly melted. Ice is but water borrowed temporarily from the sea by evaporation, and, as it built up on the land, the seabirds had to move down to the coasts in unison. Once Tasmania had departed on its slow way north, leaving deeper water in its wake, the merry-go-round of cooling Antarctic water could at last circulate freely round the continent, all the time being enriched by glacial erosion. The dissolution of Gondwana thus spawned the wonders of the Antarctic Convergence, setting the pattern of land-mass ocean currents, winds and hence climatic belts for the future.

With all the bounty of new, open oceans there for the taking, it is little wonder that both main lines of warm-blooded evolution began to take real advantage of the marine habitat, which, after all, covers five-sevenths of Planet Ocean/Earth: the penguins and the cetaceans.

The cetaceans — whales, dolphins and porpoises — are the only group of mammals that have taken entirely to the sea. The rest, the walruses, seals, sea lions and sea otters all, like the penguins, came ashore to breed.

The earliest fossil penguins come from rocks near Canterbury and date from about fifty million years ago. Another, also found in Eocene strata at Oamaru, stood 1.62 metres tall and weighed 100 kilograms. Theory has it that they may well have evolved from some sort of diving petrel. If you have ever watched a petrel trying to move about on land, you may well understand why some of them gave up the struggle and took to a life in the swim.

The cetaceans also appear to have to have turned up on the watery scene at about the same time as the penguins. So far, the earliest known fossils are from Pakistan, the fastest-moving bit of Gondwana, where hoofed mammals turned to a life browsing in the water. With no large carnivorous reptiles left in the sea, and a growing number of mammalian carnivores on the land, the sea routes were again open.

The modern whales and dolphins communicate with each other, make love, lead a family life, teach their children to sing songs, and represent a society of mind-in-water. It was they who first navigated the seas as we now know them, becoming conversant with the currents and convergences, with food stocks and the safe places in which they could bear and suckle their calves.

As the cetaceans began to make more and more use of the seas, Moa's Ark was scarcely more than a foundering hulk, and that which still showed above high-water mark was green, covered with forest and bush made up of the ancestors of many of the plants which give it greenness to this day. Much of the land as we now know it was under water, covered by shallow seas within which sediments were being laid down; sediments full of fossil information, telling us of this crucial phase of marine evolution and reminding us that the same waters that helped protect Moa's Ark from invasion were also the home port of cetacean evolution.

The isolation of Moa's Ark was, however, being threatened by this new round of Antarctic ocean circulation, which brought in many new animals to enjoy the niches of these waters. However, there was no longer any shallow-water connection: the only animals that could make the crossing were either free-swimming themselves or had a free-swimming planktonic stage in their lifecycle. In they came, new whelks and clams, mussels and oyster-like bivalves. Some came from Malaysia, some from across the Pacific, others from near-neighbour Australia and some, like *Buccinulum* and *Struthiolaria*, appear to have evolved from more local stock.

The sea routes were open, the map of the world was beginning to settle down to its present form. Coal continued to form in lowland situations such as Westland and Otago, pumping down more carbon dioxide and so, perhaps, helping the process of atmospheric cooling. New Zealand had a climate not unlike that of today's South Island. The Antarctic circulation made Moa's Ark a special place for seabirds, especially long-distance fliers.

Taiaroa Head, Otago Harbour, boasts a royal nursery, for alongside the hoiho, the people of Dunedin can show their many visitors the only mainland colony of albatrosses in the world. Like the penguins, the albatrosses and their smaller cousins the mollymawks appear to prefer the Southern Hemisphere, although a few do venture into the North Pacific. The waters around Moa's Ark are the fishing grounds of no fewer than ten sorts of these strange tube-nosed birds.

After fledging, the royal albatross spends the first five or six years at sea without touching land. During the next breeding season, it visits the breeding area, usually the same one on which it was reared. Almost as if it is reluctant to touch the land, the young bird spends much of its time circling in the air and alighting on the water. It does, however, pluck up courage and make a few test landfalls — a very descriptive term.

So, over two or three seasons, from November to March, the maturing birds become bolder and eventually display to the opposite sex. Displays vary in form and intensity, but only in the last flush of youth is the 'dance' or 'ecstatic ritual' performed. The bird stretches out its wings and rises up like a ballerina on the tips of its toes, a wonderful feat of strength and co-ordination for a bird weighing up to ten kilograms and which has spent most of its life in the air or on the water. Heads and bills are raised vertically into the sky and beaks open; screaming notes of wild

Adult royal albatross, *Diomedea epomophora*, feeding chick.
ROD MORRIS

ecstasy ring forth. Once mated, the pair are bonded for life and rarely, if ever, will they 'dance' again, the lesser displays of later years being never so ecstatic. To have witnessed this is akin to seeing Zefferelli's *Romeo and Juliet* or the first meeting of Jane and Tarzan.

The breeding, and hence 'dance', season at Taiaroa gets underway in October. It appears that the returning birds meet at a regular calendar of places — islands and peninsulas — as they make their circum-Pacific way back home. They arrive separately but already mated. The male arrives first and goes to the spot on which he first danced, or older birds go to their last nest site and may start to build, ready for the egg. Building is accomplished by the bird sitting down and then using its powerful beak to drag everything within reach of its outstretched neck, up and under itself. The nest ends up like a bell-barrow, a hump with a moat all around. Wives arrive later and, over the next month, drop in for short periods of courtship and coition. They immediately and frantically either accept the male's nest or build one of their own and lay a single, precious, white egg about nine centimetres long and weighing around 425 grams. By then, it is mid-November. The male immediately goes off to sea, returning in forty-eight hours to take over egg duty. Incubation takes between eleven and twelve weeks, and the parents swap over at weekly intervals, although there is variation. The chick takes about three days to chip out and is then fed by regurgitation, an amazing feat of food retention in a bird that may not have fed for seven days or more. The chick's eyes are open from the start, its short white down is replaced over the next forty days, when it is guarded all the time by Mum or Dad. Squid is the main food, for squids live, and albatrosses feed, at the surface. The daily feeds of the first three weeks are reduced to every two days thereafter. After the guard stage, feeding drops to around once a week.

As the chick passes its first century of days, it is resplendent in white down, each thread as long as the egg from which it hatched, a halo of silk stirred by the wind and backlit by each rising sun. In moonlight it is even more wonderful, truly a layette for a royal baby.

The next hundred days are even more critical, and the feed rate is stepped up to help the adult flight plumage to grow without blemish. For, once launched aloft, any hair-crack in the airframe could spell disaster at sea on a seven-year-long haul. Flight feathers and ailerons in place, pre-flight checks are made, wings are flexed, and landing and take-off gear is given many trials. The amount of food served by adoring parents is gradually reduced and eventually it is time for take-off.

The last chick leaves Taiaroa Head in late September and, a few days later, the next season's breeding pairs start to arrive and the whole cycle starts off with a different set of birds. There is no way that the same lot could immediately start again; they need twelve months at sea to prepare.

Should a chick die early in the nesting, the parents will return again and try the next year, but if the failure is too late in the season, this appears impossible.

People come from all around the world to see the colony and especially to witness the 'dance'. Until recently they were also hoping to catch a glimpse of Grandma, one of the grand old ladies of Taiaroa Head. First studied and banded with an ornithological ring back in 1940, she had returned to complete her royal cycle of life ever since, a life in which she must have covered at least half a million flight hours before failing to return after raising a healthy nestling in 1989. It is during those hours of flight that the Royal Class albatrosses cross and recross the Antarctic and the Tropical Convergences, no imaginary lines of navigation to them, but life-lines of rich productivity, zones of congregation and celebration.

The Southern Ocean is the body of water surrounding Antarctica: The Convergence, at a mean radius of 2,400 miles from the Pole, marks its northern limit, with major concentrations of krill between it and the frozen continent. Krill, *Euphausia superba*, is a sort of free-swimming shrimp, growing to about seven centimetres long. Krill feeds directly on the plant plankton, and itself directly feeds even the greatest of the whales, the blue whale, the largest mammal that has ever lived. It thus plays a key role in the exuberance of life in these cold seas, for its compound eyes allow it to see and thus browse the tiny plankton, and it grows large enough to be seen and hence to succour squid, fish, penguins, other seabirds and baleen whales. Baleen whales are those with rakers made of baleen, which screen the krill out of each great gulp of ready-salted gazpacho soup and allow the mammals to grow blubber and bask in their own inner warmth. The main food chains are thus kept short; only the sperm

A group of Hector's dolphins, *Cephalorhynchus hectori*.
STEVE DAWSON

Plastic non-rot net, the scourge of the seas.

whales, their toothed kin, and carnivores like leopard seals feed at the fourth level, and so are perforce much rarer denizens of the floating deep. For at each step in any chain of energy change there is massive loss of potential, and the higher up the chain, the rarer will your lifestyle be.

Recently, the largest school of krill ever tracked was found near Elephant Island, off the Antarctic Peninsula. It took up several square kilometres of sea, descended to 200 metres and was estimated to contain about 10,000 tonnes — one-seventh of the annual world catch of all marine fish. Productivity indeed! No wonder the great whales, together with the crab-eater, Weddell, leopard, Ross, southern and fur seals, the penguins, fulmars, petrels, cormorants, skuas, terns and gulls in their millions, share the waters of the Southern Ocean with the royal albatross.

From the cold Antarctic to the heat of the tropics, Grandma winged her way for at least fifty years, restocking her egg batteries ready for the next laying. Over her lifetime she saw certain nations of the world come to their senses and stop the wanton slaughter of the whales. She saw the attempts of many nations to persuade themselves that they may harvest the krill to their own ends, leaving little for the rest of nature's food chain. She saw the destruction of so much forest land on the islands of the Pacific and the mainlands surrounding it that some of her feeding grounds, though enriched, are so tainted with eroded silt that she could scarcely see to feed even at the surface.

Every two years on her way back home to Taiaroa, Grandma increasingly missed the distinctive low-spout greeting of one of the world's smallest cetaceans, Hector's dolphin. Feeding as it does in the wet dock of Moa's Ark, and especially in and off her estuaries, Hector's dolphin has fallen prey to fishing nets in ever greater numbers. In recent years catches have increased, not only in nets set to catch their fishy prey but also in the thousands of kilometres of nets that have broken free from their moorings and, lost, have drifted out to sea. There, untended and uncharted, they have become pelagic graveyards of vast proportions, entangling first carcases, then, in time, white-washed skeletons of fish, fowl and mammals, which dance a macabre dance of death forever. For the new plastic net and monofilament lines do not rot, they remain an obscenity of modern invention. Hector's dolphin is on the brink, the very edge of extinction — can New Zealanders be sufficiently self-less to save this unique little large mammal?

Punakaiki Pancakes

Moa's Ark, as if tethered to Australia on a line too long for even the most adventurous land mammal to cross, moved northward, away from the cooling Antarctic. At the same time, Malaysia, Indonesia and the Philippines were rotating south, closing the gap with Papua New Guinea and Australia until the latter two, the largest island and the smallest continent in the world, became, to all intents and migration purposes, one land mass. The gradually closing contact of the island groups funneled tropical currents down to meet Moa's Ark, warming its northern waters and opening up links with the northern continents, on which evolution had been going its own way towards domination by the true mammals. These included efficient plant-eaters, like the ancestors of our modern elephants, antelopes, horses, cattle and sheep, all of which have teeth that grow throughout their lifetime. Without teeth to grind its food, a herbivore will die, unable to eat the rough, tough leaves and twigs, so non-stop tooth growth was an important evolutionary step.

Not only was the climate of Antarctica changing, but the new, distinctly zoned climatic belts of the world were widening and becoming fixed. The west-wind bias brought droughts to areas distant from the sea, and especially to those on the eastern flanks of new mountain chains, places where there was insufficient water for trees to grow, and so the grasses and annual plants took over. It was at this time that the first monkey-like primates moved mindfully through the dwindling forests of the world and peered out at the rolling grasslands on which enormous herds of ungulates were grazing.

Moa's Ark itself was beginning a period of refit. Earthquakes began to shake the forest-clad plains. Coal was still being laid down in great deltas, made of the old products of erosion as new ridges of land began to rise up from the sea. New, embryonic mountain chains emerged, those to the north of Auckland being flanked by active volcanoes.

The first tropical arrivals were marine organisms, which could float on the warm currents, and soon the northern shores right down to East Cape were fringed with molluscs akin to modern sting cone shells and *Murex*, and the strange shells of nautiloids were washed up upon the strand. It always seems a shame that the great ammonites and belemnites did not survive through to modern times, and we can only wonder why. We are, however, fortunate still to have tusk shells, nautiloids and the paper nautilus to remind us that they, like the squids and octopi, are in fact intelligent, free-swimming snails.

The shorelines of these northern lands also had more than a tropical feel about them. With sea temperatures 5 to 7°C warmer than today, there would have been no need to cross the Tasman to expose yourself in Brisbane or live it up at Surfers'

Flowering toetoe, *Cortaderia fulvida*.

A cabbage tree, *Cordyline australis*, near Lake Wanaka.

Paradise and the sun-traps north along the Barrier Reef. Moa's Ark had its own groves of coconut palm trees.

Palms, cordylines and grasses are all members of the great group of flower-bearing plants called the monocotyledons, because they all have only one seed leaf, or cotyledon. All the rest usually have two. The vast majority of them also have narrow, grass-like leaves and rather inconspicuous flowers, which are pollinated by the wind. The fruits of grasses are one-seeded nutlets. Usually they are very light and remain joined to at least part of the dry, papery flower. The whole acts like a parachute and is carried away by the wind, or the scales are serrated so that they catch on passing animals. Some have special food stores which attract ants and other insects to carry them away. Grasses are thus very adept at moving about, and that's how Moa's Ark must have obtained the ancestors of its famous tussock grasses, para-hopping along the island chains.

In much the same way came the coconuts and the cabbage trees, not wafted on the wind, but rafted on the sea, thanks to their ability to float. And while on the subject of rafting, trees falling into the sea and pieces of swamp and other vegetation flushed out to sea by floods can carry not only the seeds of plants but great lumps of soil, complete with many smaller animals. So they too may traverse vast distances by riding the ocean currents. Likewise a floating log, a vegetation raft or even an iceberg can act as a resting place for storm-driven birds and insects.

The famous Pancake Rocks at Punakaiki will open our eyes onto this Oligocene window of around 24 million years ago. At about that time the Pancake Rocks had already been formed. They are made of limestone that was laid down in very still

A stack of pancake rocks, Punakaiki.

104

waters, for there are no pebbles and larger bits to break up the perfection of their many layers — layers made up of multi-mega-trillions of skeletons of tiny animals called foramenifera and even smaller lime-secreting plant plankton. The Pancake Rocks as we see them today are the harder, less lime-rich ones, which have not been eroded and swept away by the sea. When you have witnessed the power of waves driven by the westerlies into the surge pools and blowholes, you will marvel at the strength of these rocks.

Like all the visitors, I was drawn by the dull thuds and thumps and the hissing, roaring noises, down along the tracks to stand, mouth open, tasting salt as spray and spume cascaded up into the air. A high sea was running and the thwack of the enormous waves against the pancake bastions, sending up pressure waves of air, reminded me of the blast from the biggest bombs that fell in wartime London.

I marvelled at the anchoring ability of the aptly named bull kelp and at its shiny slipperiness which allows its fronds to slide and swirl across the rocks apparently without damage. Then an extra large wave sent one kelp plant, which must have been dislodged, up the Chimney Pot, the best of the blowholes. The large, brown seaweed stood erect some twenty metres into the air and was cheered by a crowd of tourists, all of whom got soaked into the bargain.

What a spectacle! And for millions of years there was no one to appreciate it. The gulls and white-fronted terns were certainly enjoying the wind punching up the cliffs, and both blue and spotted shags were fishing offshore. What is more, not far away is the only mainland colony of the rare Westland black petrel, discovered as recently as 1945 by pupils from the school at Barrytown. Petrels are relatives of the albatrosses and, like them and the headland of Punakaiki, they too have tubes on their beaks. Despite the fact that they build nests in burrows, they are very clumsy when on the ground, but are masters of the marine airways. The modern diving petrels are birds of inshore waters and spend much of their time bobbing and floating on the waves between short, whirring, just-above-the-surface flights. Crash-diving into the water, they use their wings to fly along in search of fish and squid, emerging to bob, penguin-like, not far from the foot of the roaring cliffs. They, like all other seabirds, must enjoy life around the Pancake Rocks, for if they didn't they could just up and fly away.

The tour parties, of course, have to do just that, their coach drivers and couriers calling them on to the other delights of this section of coast and far beyond. As they walk back up the tracks from the blowholes through the monocotyledons, flax, cabbage trees and nikau (New Zealand's only native palm) growing in impossible places on the very edge of the roaring cliffs, it all has a very tropical look and feel. Yet there, in those same places, you can see the little blue penguins making their own dogged way up to their nest sites, giving a polar flavour and linking the two extremes of the climate of Moa's Ark.

A trip to Cape Foulwind to the north links us back through many of the earlier windows of evolutionary time, for there in the cliff section can be seen coarse-grained granite rocks. These were formed by the slow cooling of Paleozoic magma 430 million years ago. As the waves draw back from the foot of the cliffs, it is like an eyelid of time revealing past ages when only simple animals like sponges were

Grove of nikau palms, *Rhopalostylis sapida*, near Punakaiki.

Flowers of the nikau palm.

Foam on the beach, Punakaiki.

around — and there they are, bright red and orange, almost unchanged through such an immensity of time.

All along that stretch of coast another strange phenomenon can be seen and enjoyed, but this requires both preparation and debriefing. When the conditions are right, mountains of froth and foam roll in with every wave, covering the beaches and especially the enclosed bays to a depth of several metres. This strange phenomenon has nothing to do with pollution, in fact it is a natural product of one of the world's purest and most natural landscapes, drawn from both land and sea. From the land comes a solution of history, natural chemicals dissolved from the forest soil and made of the remains of mosses, tree ferns, podocarps and flowering plants that still clothe the adjacent Paparoa Mountains. This gold-tinted tincture of natural history mixes and mingles with the abundant slippums that protect the kelps and other seaweeds from abrasion, to produce a natural detergent-like complex which is beaten into foam.

To enjoy nature's own bubblebath you must don your togs and brave the elements. We did just that while filming, and the whole crew was engulfed in this amazing, popping, bubbling tsunami of foam. Like all detergents, it picks up and holds all manner of things — in this case you can't call it dirt, for these are some of New Zealand's cleanest beaches, and New Zealand can boast some of the cleanest in the world. The foam load includes not only plants and animal plankton, all far too small to see with the naked eye, but also tiny bits of debris and fine silt, which ends up all over you. That's why debriefing must include a swim in foam-free sea to rid yourself of an all-over tide mark. Not an easy thing to do when even the rock pools are capped with foam. But never fear, in many places well above high-water mark there are pools of crystal-clear water draining from the limestone. The water is, of course, much colder than the sea and so is ideal for waking you up to the realities of life when you have been bathing in history.

108

A Day on Bald Mountain

If by this time you are getting fed up with stories about plants and animals, then a good place to go is Mount Baldy, for, as its name implies, nothing much appears to grow on its flanks.

Mount Baldy is part of the Craigieburn Range and rises to 1,700 metres. Like many of the other mountains of the north of the South Island, it is made of grey-wacke, a name that proves geologists have a sense of humour. Greywacke is a rather coarse, bluish or greenish sandstone, originally laid down in the sea, but during the last five million years it has been thrust up to form these jumbled mountain chains, many of which have risen into the frosty, rock-shattering alpine zone only during the last million years. The same is true for much of the present superstructure of Moa's Ark, even the volcanoes of the north. Ruapehu is probably the oldest, for the first eruptions there took place no more than two million years ago. Ngauruhoe is the youngest: developing only over the past two to three thousand years. It is 2,290 metres

Looking east from Mount Baldy to the distant Canterbury Plains.

The Mount Baldy buttercup, *Ranunculus haastii*.

in height, not a bad effort for one so young. As these high spots have been put in place, so too have they been eroded away, and only in the south-west and in the Tasman Mountains are the hills made of more durable hard rocks like granite.

So, despite the fact that our next window on the world of the Pliocene is young, it is also bald. Well, not quite, as a visit to its frost-shattered screes will show. It is a case of three steps up and two back, all the way to the top, with many rests in between to take in the view and the local vegetation. Watch where you put your feet, especially when you are scree-running, the easiest and most exciting way back to the bottom.

The Mount Baldy or Haast buttercup is one of the commonest plants of the high slopes, although it cannot be called abundant, but it is there clinging with you onto the eroding scree. The plant finds this downsliding life much to its liking. Rooted deep in the damp soil beneath the running rocks, its fleshy, food-packed rhizome grows downslope, popping up as the will takes it, to produce a rosette of waxy blue-green leaves, which are almost invisible amongst the greywacke. A waxy yellow flower gives its position away, but the flower soon fades and is replaced by precious fruit. The strange penwiper plant is another scree denizen whose large fleshy root stores food down in the soil beneath the loose rock. A member of the mustard flower family, its many strongly scented creamy flowers are clustered into a single head. Only the large plants bloom, and when they have set seed they die. On a world scale, plants with black flowers are a rarity; however, Mount Baldy boasts one, the black button daisy. Rooting deep in the soil, its branching stems bear thick, fleshy, feathery leaves and little round black button flowers with yellow stamens.

If black flowers are rare in any habitat, then willowherbs are common on many mountains and, not to be outdone, Mount Baldy puts on a good show of the thick-stemmed species. This is one of a number of plants that have a rather strange distribution: widespread on the mountains of the South Island, they have outlier populations in the Ruahine Mountains, which provide a backdrop to the Manawatu in the south of the North Island. The Ruahines are also very young, and less than four million years ago a seaway stretched from Taranaki and Wanganui eastward across the present site of the Ruahines, from the Manawatu Gorge northward to the Napier–Taupo road and out into much deeper water covering what is now Hawke's Bay. Strong tidal currents flowing through this seaway, driven by the westerlies, kept the old, harder basement rocks clear of silt and sand, allowing immense beds of barnacles to grow for thousands upon thousands of years. Barnacles are not molluscs but a strange sort of armour-plated shrimp that cements itself to the rock with its head and kicks food into its mouth with its legs. They thrive on rocks between the tides and, before the development of fast ships and highly toxic antifouling paints, used to encrust the hulls of watercraft from the Plimsoll line down. The armour plates of the massive growths of barnacles, which once encrusted a large section of the midships of Moa's Ark, may now be seen very high and dry, a thousand metres up the flanks of the Ruahines.

Mount Baldy and both its younger and older brethren thus bring us face to face with the enigma of New Zealand's alpine plants. Whence did they come to colonise these new penthouse suites? It must be remembered that, for at least fifty million

Mountain willowherb, *Epilobium crassum*.

Common on scree slopes — *Stellaria roughii*.

Speargrasses, or spaniards, like the well-named *Aciphylla horrida*, are common on the mountains.

At home in the Alps,
Ourisia macrophylla.

The mountain daisy, *Celmisia verbascifolia*, is a common alpine plant.

years before the upheavals of the Miocene and Pliocene periods, Moa's Ark was a flat, eroded hulk with few, if any, of its timbers rising up to be shivered and shattered by the alpine zone. What is more, the climate was warmer than it is today. New Zealand has no less than 600 alpine plants, of that there is no doubt. How did they get onto the Ark, this impressive muster of beauties, no fewer than ninety-three per cent of which are endemic? Even more remarkable is the fact that the alpine flora clinging to the mastheads of Moa's Ark contains several genera, eight to be exact, that are also endemic, and another fifteen that have only a few of their species outside New Zealand. All this home-base endemicity suggests a long history of alpine conditions, which is certainly not the case.

Some, like the gentians and willowherbs, have been on the Ark since the Pliocene, for they have left their pollen ingrained in the fossil memory-banks to prove it. The pollen of other modern-day alpinists dates back much further, indicating that they were here and doing well in the warm flatlands. Inferences, if not conclusions, must then be drawn that the vast majority of New Zealand's alpine plants have evolved *in situ* from lowland species and genera.

The mountains of today not only provide a home for the alpines, but they also gather and hold the long white cloud which gave Aotearoa its name. Like the cloud, these were also the places which gathered and held the snow that formed the generation centres of glaciers and local ice ages. Warmth-demanding species would have been pushed further and further downslope as the ice built up. Some would have become extinct, others wiped out from certain sections of the land, while the lucky ones could have moved out onto what had been areas of continental shelf before the earth's expanding icecaps locked up the water, causing the sea levels to fall. So new territory was opened up, meaning new opportunities for plants that had in their genetic make-up the information allowing them to survive under colder, more frosty conditions. There was a premium for plants (and insects) able to tolerate shorter growing periods. As the pendulum swung back and warm interglacial conditions reasserted themselves, the whole process was reversed as the new alpinists climbed the hills, the first unchallenged colonists of wide-open mountain habitats. The warmth-demanding bush and forest plants came out of their warm, especially favoured hiding places to take over what lowland situations were left as sea level rose, chasing the alpinists up the hills, squeezing them into smaller and smaller isolated areas on the highest slopes and peaks.

A series of ice ages of varying intensity, interspersed with warm periods of different lengths and different intensities, would thus have provided ideal conditions to stimulate a real genetic shake-up of alpine opportunities, a series of package-deal holidays on the slopes or down by the sea, speeding evolution.

Proof is added to this presumptuous pudding by the fact that, like the willowherb of the Ruahines and the Southern Alps, a number of New Zealand's alpine plants show disjunctions in their distributions. Most famous are a whole group of alpine plants found on the heights around Nelson and in Fiordland but nowhere in between. One or two may have made the long-distance hop, but if so, why aren't at least some of them found on mountains in between ideally suited to their lifestyle? The most satisfying explanation so far is that they were all at one time much more widespread

Castle Hill, looking west towards the Craigieburn Range.

The Castle Hill buttercup reserve.

Mount Cook lily, or great mountain buttercup,
Ranunculus lyallii.

and that during one or more warm interglacials, were wiped out at all lower stations in between. Surviving only in these far-separated massifs, they simply climbed back up to the top of the mountains, forced into high alpine isolation by the invasion of bush and forest on the lower slopes as the ice age came to an end.

This story of survival is highlighted as you descend the winding road from Mount Baldy towards the Canterbury Plains. Surrounded by foothills of greywacke is Castle Hill, a mere 920 metres high, rising from the Trelissick Basin. It is studded with limestone tors, a term of Cornish derivation. John and Charles Enys, the second owners of the property, arrived in New Zealand from Cornwall, an English county famed for its blocks of stone standing alone in the landscape.

Around the tors of Castle Hill there are strange patches of lime-rich ground, white and crystalline, which reflect the energy of the sun and quickly drain rainwater away, much like the screes on Mount Baldy. Amongst the loose materials can be found what looks like the Baldy buttercup; but on closer inspection it is a very different plant and is indeed the rarest buttercup in the world, named after Castle Hill, the only place in which it grows. What is even more exciting, it is not alone, for there in the well-drained and very unstable habitat are a number of other plants of the true alpine zone. They were left behind to sweat it out as the glaciers melted and warmth spread over the lowland plains. The alpines were thus banished from the plains and the foothills, shaded out by developing forest except in these small patches of lime-rich gravel, which are so unstable that lowland shrubs could never gain a firm foothold.

New Zealand's most famous buttercup also ranks in the record book, for the great mountain buttercup is the largest in the world. It is widespread through all the wetter mountains of South and Stewart Islands and is the logo of Mount Cook Airlines. It is nice to have two major airlines in one country with a botanical logo, but, of course, New Zealand is a very important place for plants.

Looking through the tally of no less than fourteen buttercups listed as always occurring on the mountains, nine of them show marked disjunctions in their distribution and some have ended up really out on a limb, isolated in one tiny area. The Godley District buttercup is found only high in the central Southern Alps; the snow buttercup warms its feet mainly on the high volcanic areas of the north; while the Mount Cook buttercup opens its flowers only on a tiny area of New Zealand's highest peak.

Anything the buttercups can do, so too can the daisies. The daisy family has also taken to the ski slopes, and no fewer than 113 species have entered the alpine lists. Apart from the snow tussocks, which are grasses, one genus of plants really tells you that you have arrived high on the masts of Moa's Ark. The genus is *Celmisia* and that too is their common name, and although only thirty-six of the native celmisias are described as alpine, fifty out of sixty of the mainland species reach the alpine zone.

The Sky-Piercer

New Zealand's highest mountain (known as Aoraki to the Kai Tahu people), another must on any grand tour of Moa's Ark, boasts not only an airline named after it with the world's biggest buttercup on its tail, but also an icy summit where time has stood still, frozen solid, for at least 20,000 years. Like the demise of the dinosaurs, which took some 60 million years, the development of the Great Ice Age was also a slow business. What is more, the two events are not unconnected.

While the dinosaurs were still thriving and were heading towards Moa's Ark, the world's land masses were lining themselves up into a new pattern which pointed towards the big freeze. Throughout the following period, coal, lignite and peat were being laid down in various parts of the world, trees were growing tall, and deep humus-rich forest soils were developing over vast areas. Likewise, in the sea, reefs forming limestone and chalk were widespread, the limestone made of the remains of corals and shells and the chalk made up of the tiny skeletons of planktonic plants called coccoliths. All this live action was removing carbon dioxide from the atmosphere and dumping it in long-term store, thereby helping to turn the earth's greenhouse thermostat down to cool. These were not ideal conditions for the ruling reptile classes. Then, around forty-five million years ago, the main switch was turned off and the world moved into reflective mood. Ice grew apace on Antarctica, and continents with high mountains began to form a ring at the other end of the world which would almost landlock the Arctic Ocean.

By the end of the Pliocene, about two million years ago, the world's climates had really taken a turn for the worse; or for the better if you happened to be an ultra-adaptable, ready-to-seize-every-opportunity buttercup, daisy or human being. By this time our ancestors, in the shape of *Homo habilis*, were doing well in the warmth of tropical Africa. For the next 1,550,000 years numerous ice ages began to shiver the timbers of the world and of Moa's Ark, the major effect being felt in the circumpolar, temperate and subtropical zones.

Far beyond the limit of the ice, weather patterns changed and climates shifted, and so did the zones of vegetation. Back and forth they went, climbing up and down the hills or moving from shady to sunny slopes and back, as the ice ages waxed and waned. Soils that had become stabilised, impoverished and soured over long periods of time were rejuvenated as the roots of the new immigrant plants pushed deeper and added new sorts of litter, worms and insects to the process of soil formation. Some oldsters who could not change their ways and move with the times, died out. Others, both young and old, took advantage of the new opportunities and developed arctic, alpine, montane and even maritime races. For, as the ice built up upon the mountains, the sea level went down in unison.

Mounts Cook, or Aoraki (3,746 metres), and Tasman (3,498 metres), still in the grip of the Ice Age.
LLOYD HOMER, NZ GEOLOGICAL SURVEY

It was an ultra-slow-motion cycle of change, but severely affected all the inhabitants of Moa's Ark. No wonder the penguins had done so well down at sea level and the alpine plants had kitted themselves out ready for the real winter sports, which began only 850,000 years ago. For, from that point on, at least eight more ice ages, each one deeper and longer than the last, began to change the world. It would appear that by the time the Antarctic continent was covered with at least 22,500 million million tonnes of ice and the Arctic Ocean was frozen over, glaciers were gathering on many mountains, and icebergs and pack ice were spreading both north and south, cooling the seas and sending frigid winds through the temperate zones towards the subtropics. Temperature-wise, if the glacial lows were lower, the interglacial highs (or at least some of them) were higher, and the climate of Moa's Ark, even at deck level, fluctuated between cold subpolar and warm subtropical, for unmistakable signs of kauri forest may be found as far south as Wellington. (While Wellington had its kauri forest, London enjoyed the presence of lions, hippopotami and the like; an interglacial tropical paradise.)

What exactly causes the fluctuation in the ice-age scenario and makes the temperature go up and down is still something of a mystery. The fine-tuning of the global winter could well be due to the greenhouse effect, for as the ice sheets advance, much vegetation is destroyed, releasing carbon dioxide on a massive scale. Likewise, shoals and reefs are exposed as the sea levels retreat; they decay, again releasing carbon dioxide. In consequence, the atmosphere warms and the process is reversed as the greenhouse gas is locked up once more. Fine-tuning indeed, for the overall temperature difference between full glacial and full interglacial is only 14°C. Fine-tuning on a massive scale, for the figure refers to average global temperature and at the height of the last glacial, only 15,000 years ago, nearly thirty per cent of the earth's surface was covered with ice, compared with ten per cent today. A staggering difference of thirty million square kilometres of land scoured clean of vegetation! If that had been only scrub forest, its destruction could have increased the atmospheric concentration of carbon dioxide by twenty per cent — enough to trigger the next warm phase; enough to speed the rate of photosynthesis on the new alpine tundra and grassland communities rearranging themselves on land, and the new swamps and forests growing on the exposed parts of the continental shelves.

What a mess! But also, what a stir-up for the soils! As we shall see, they really needed it. Add to this the fact that the glacial-interglacial tuning was never spot-on, and the main ups and downs were attenuated with smaller blips and bloops called stadials and interstadials.

In order to take our look at this turmoil of arctic alpineness, all we need do is go to Mount Cook and its periglacial surroundings. There are many approaches to this ice-rimmed window of time, the most elegant being to join the jet set of skiers at the Hermitage for a flight by ski-plane, complete with great buttercup logo, up to one of the glaciers. To go this way is a bit of a cheat, for such scenic flights are only possible on those duck-egg-blue-full-of-sunshine-interstadial days.

To go through the ice-window for real, the best way is to join a tramping, climbing party, complete with guide and all the gear, and make a crossing of the Southern Alps. En route you must, and probably will, meet two birds that have benefited from the ups and downs of the ice ages. All around the Hermitage or your campsite your ears will be assailed by the far-reaching cry of *Nestor notabilis*, the kea. Take note of an olive-green parrot with a red underwing which flashes as it flies away. If you want to meet an omnivore, you are about to, for the kea eats almost everything — insects and plants in all stages of their life and death cycle, carrion, sandwiches, both the filling and the bread — so they will come to very close quarters wherever you stop for lunch.

Parrots on high mountains in the cold are a remarkable sight. They enjoy flying in the face of high winds, and even manage to roll in the snow, attracting your attention and your last sandwich. Do not give it to them, for you are going to need all the energy you can muster to climb up and over the ranges; they can fly down to the forest edge, where there is plenty of their natural food. Like so many other large-beaked birds that are seen feeding on carrion, the kea has gained a reputation as a killer of lambs and was on the wanted dead, not alive, list. It is a totally undeserved reputation, and to kill a kea is an act of wanton resourcicide. Anyone who would disagree must take note that if there were one-tenth the number of

The cheeky kea, *Nestor notabilis*, camping out.
ROD MORRIS

tourists visiting New Zealand as there are resident sheep, then New Zealand would be one of the richest countries in the world. To prove it, the 857,000 foreign tourists who visited the country in 1987, many of whom took home cherished snapshots of keas, earned more than half the foreign exchange netted by the whole agricultural industry.

As you ascend through the valleys, the alpine plants do their best to hide the rocks, shattered and scoured by ice-age conditions, and the strange vegetable sheep remind us that plants, even when bearing the name of animals, hold and stabilise the eroded rocks, nursing them back into productive life. A whole complex of plants are found in the mountains, all of which grow in the form of large, swelling cushions, and when their leaves terminate in long white hairs, the whole mass looks like a sheep lying on the rocks. Many of this flock of monster vegetables belong to the genus *Raoulia*, another member of the daisy flower family that has become one of the après-scree set and gives the alpine zone of Moa's Ark a character all of its own.

Amongst the sheep, vegetable and vegetarian, the gentians, buttercups, forget-me-nots, spear grasses and eyebrights, you may be lucky enough to meet New Zealand's only true alpine bird, a bird which does not retreat down to the forest at the onset of winter. How such a tiny bird as the rock wren manages to keep warm through the alpine winter is a mystery. The vegetable sheep may help, for the bird appears to lead a semi-troglodytic life, snuggling up to *Raoulia* beneath a protective blanket of snow. The rock wren has been a passenger on Moa's Ark for millions of years. It builds an igloo-like nest complete with entrance tunnel and a central nest

Two vegetable sheep species growing on the Waimakariri riverbed.

chamber, all woven from the snow tussock grasses. The chamber is lined with feathers when they are available, and when they are in short supply, the down of lichens and moss suffices.

This tiny bird leads you on across a lesson in periglacial geomorphology, showing the way in which the action of the ice age eroded the rocks and moulded the landscapes. Flitting from rock to rock, the bird draws your attention to some that are polished and scoured by the passing of the ice masses, and others still in their frost-shattered state, waiting for some vegetable sheep to put down its roots.

Then, ice axes and crampons at the ready and the party well roped up, proceed onto the glaciers themselves, past their crevassed snouts where the jumble of collapsing rock and ice is too dangerous to approach. Each glacier has a living heart or generation zone, where the excess of snowfall over snowmelt turns the softness of new snow feathers into hard-packed ice. The whole, ever-increasing weight pushes the glacier downslope to scour the valleys below, creating the fiords of the future. From the top, on a clear day, you can see down to the sea where, at the height of the glaciation, the glaciers met the tides running in over a much wider coastal plain.

En route down the western side of the Divide (and it is not an easy one), you skirt through one of the wonders of the living world: mixed podocarp and beech forest growing cheek by jowl with living ice. Nowhere else in the world is there better proof of the tenacity of forest to hang onto the old or rapidly recolonise new ground in the face or the wake of an ice age. There too, between the ice and the forest fringe, are the alpines taking their chance of survival. Kauri and tropical soil around Wellington in the not-too-far-distant past, and here are nikau palms and penguins not far from the snout of the Fox Glacier.

Franz Josef

Time may have stood still and frozen solid on the top of Mount Cook and the other snow-capped peaks, but time is very fluid in the valleys that drain their flanks. Our next time window slides open below the Franz Josef Glacier, for, as the last glaciation went into decline, ice action has withdrawn up the valley of the Waiho River, leaving new landscapes open for recolonisation and soil formation. The whole sequence, from the foot of the glaciers to the sea, is best regarded as a timed record, the gradual changes being written in the intricate beauty of the vegetation and the living soil which now covers the once bare rock.

The contemporary climate is mild and very wet, with some 4,000 to 5,000 millimetres of rain in each and every average year. The soils that have been and are being formed on the flood plain of the river have the same parentage: coarse grey alluvium prepared by the glacier and well sorted by melt water. The soil sequence is conveniently arranged in five broad steps, each marking a major phase of glacial retreat, each older than the last, together reaching back through post-glacial time. In order to locate them in sequence downstream, we will name each terrrace after the soil type which dominates that age.

The glacier recently retreated and, close to its snout, exposed the river flats of the youngest terrace, with Hokitika soils, somewhere between twenty-five and 100 years ago. Today, they are still part bare and part covered with mats of moss and flocks of vegetable sheep, a more or less open community which grades downstream through *Olearia* scrub to pioneer hardwood forest, the latter being especially well developed where the alluvium gives way to roche moutonne. The French term refers to rocks which have been rounded and polished by glacial action so that they look like — well, count them for yourself, but do not go to sleep, for there are many more exciting things to see.

By the time you get to the next terrace, with Ikamatua soils, the riverbed has been clear of ice for 500 years, the process of colonisation and succession is complete and the terraces are becoming covered with tall mixed forest. Kamahi and rata are doing particularly well, every tree reaching up to the cloudy sky.

Now you must put on your seven-league boots, for the next step back in time takes you to the Waiuta soils, on a terrace which has been free of ice for at least 5,000 years. The forest is becoming tall and dense and the golden bronze of tall rimu has joined the dark green of the rata in emerging above the canopy of kamahi and other hardwoods. Then on down to a magnificent 11,000-year-old terminal moraine known as the Waiho loop, where the Kumara soils show a bleached horizon and tall rimu dominates the overstorey.

Nothing has changed here except the soils, the forest is still in its natural state, unlogged and unburned, only another 6,000 years of time has taken its toll.

Unfortunately, older tracts of forest which once existed lower down the course of the Waiho have been lost, flooded by the post-glacial return of the sea to its present level. In order to find out what happens to forest ecosystems after 11,000 years of development, we must deviate a little to the Okarito soils in the old alluvium which cap the Omoeroa Range of hills. There, a rather desolate, though beautiful and immensely interesting sight meets your eyes — a bonsai forestscape of stunted yellow and silver pines and heathland, or pakihi, vegetation. Quite a shock, especially when you consider that there have been no fires, no volcanic eruptions, no acid rain to help trigger the change. This degraded landscape is the end point of natural processes of ecological change which have taken about 25,000 years to complete. A long time for us humans, but a mere blink in the voyage time of Moa's Ark. So how did it come about?

Study of the soil gives us at least part of an explanation. At the glacier's snout, the effects of glaciation are all too obvious — raw rock pulverised by ice and redistributed by melt water, the bare bones of a cold habitat in which only the toughest pioneer plants and animals can make a living. Soil formation is in its infancy.

One hundred years later, and downriver the soil is still in its early stages of development, full of mineral promise, with important nutrients like phosphate and potassium becoming available to plant roots and recycled each year by leaf and litter fall, back and forth from soil to vegetation. Likewise, plenty of bases, bicarbonates of calcium and magnesium and salts of iron, are in circulation, warding off the detrimental effects of acidification. No need for top-dressing or the application of agricultural lime! The vegetable sheep have done their best, adding humus and structure to the soil and feeding an ever-richer soil fauna, so that other plants and animals are able to join the process of succession and soil formation.

After 5,000 years, the top twenty centimetres of the soils is suffused with a red-brown colouration. Leaching by rain and the acid products of the vegetation have eaten into the ground-up particles of rock, releasing minerals and nutrients. Some of these have been taken up into the cycle of vegetation growth, but others, like iron, have been washed down through the soil, giving it its rusty red colour. The process of plant succession is almost complete, with mature forest growing on a still-rich soil, with well-marked horizons, or layers: dark humus, rich at the top, well leached and paler down below, with a concentration of rust-red iron salts and other minerals even deeper.

In time, where the watertable rising up meets the water washing down, a layer, or iron pan, becomes so hardened that the plant roots can no longer reach down to the mineral-rich alluvium below, and even the drainage of water becomes impeded. It is a pattern which appears to hold steady for the next 5,000 or so years, backed up by recycling and the further release of minerals from the upper parts of the soil profile. The main changes are an intensification of the leached and the iron-rich layers and an increase in the likelihood of waterlogging of the soils and stress of the trees owing to mineral deficiencies.

From this point on, it all appears to be downhill. In the Omoeroa Range, the

A river of ice — the Franz Josef Glacier.
NEVILLE PEAT

Snout of the Franz Josef Glacier.
DEPARTMENT OF CONSERVATION

rooting layers have lost much of their organic nitrogen, phosphorus is unavailable to plant growth, acidity is increased and other minerals are lost from the profile. No wonder the trees take on bonsai form, for up to ninety per cent of the nutrients which put the gloss on the flocks of vegetable sheep, which pioneered the way of soil development, have been lost from circulation.

The actual picture is, of course, not that simple, for 22,000 years ago the environment of Okarito was certainly not cool temperate, and since that time a number of marked fluctuations in both temperature and rainfall have helped things on their way. Neither can this simplistic picture of soil development be applied to all areas of New Zealand, for they are blessed or cursed by much harder, less erodable rocks, less rain and warmer or cooler temperatures.

Soil profile under pakihi.
QUENTIN CHRISTIE

Pakihi vegetation with *Gahnia* tussocks, near Okarito.

However, the message is there, written firmly on the slips along the sides of the Waiho Valley. Soils and their vegetation are not static entities, they are dynamic, living systems, which change all the time. An important part of that process of change is nutrient loss, soil and vegetation degradation and, in areas where leaching is the major component of soil formation, the development of acidity, processes as inexorable as time itself.

So what would New Zealand and the world have been like if there had been no series of glaciations to stir things up? No grinding-up of rocks, carving of new valleys and re-sorting of new landscapes? No advance and retreat of ice, forest, grassland and heath, only the slow processes of natural detrimental change? What sort of a world would have been there to meet the onslaught of a change more far-reaching than the most severe of all the glaciations, the appearance of *Homo sapiens*?

It was at the height of the last glaciation that the first people moved from Eurasia into North and then South America. Also, people moved from the mainland of Malaysia down through the islands of Indonesia into Australia, which at that time was re-welded into the South-East Asian land mass by glacial drawdown of the ocean waters. Only Moa's Ark was spared this final invasion of its wilderness, until well into the Holocene, the present past — or is it? For there is, indeed, no proof that the world has shaken off the frosts of the ice ages that have dominated the climates of the lower and higher latitudes and altitudes for the last one million years. In fact, the first people only invaded the sanctity of Moa's Ark as the vegetable sheep took up residence on the river flats below the site of the present-day Ikamatua soils, some thousand years ago.

Franz Josef was an emperor who, like Queen Victoria, came to the throne young and reigned through the whole restructuring of Europe. The glacier that bears his name has done the same for the whole restructuring of the living landscapes of Moa's Ark, and many of the unique residents of New Zealand, both plants and animals, have come within its sphere of influence — shuffling and seeding their way both south and north along the coast, expanding and contracting their ranges up, down and across slopes, and along the chronosequence to gain survival and seize new opportunities. All part and parcel of the process of creative evolution.

By the time the Waiuta terrace was being colonised, the world's sea levels had crept back to their present levels. The world's map was much as it is today, for although the continents were, and still are, on the move, the time-scale is too short to appreciate their movement. All those lands no longer burdened by ice are rising, the earth's elastic crust heaving a sigh of relief, and others are see-sawing down and disappearing below the waves. New forests, swamps and peatlands have been busy mopping up the carbon dioxide and packing it away in long-term store. The British Isles are islands once more, already colonised by farmers who worked stone, cleared land and planted crops. The vastness of Amazonas, much of which had been covered with grasslands during at least some parts of the ice age, is under its panoply of tropical rainforest. Moa's Ark rides high, 4,000 years away from discovery by human minds, although in about AD 186 the then-civilised world was going to record the impact of the place.

Pureora and the Big Sneeze

This window could equally well be called 'Pureora and the Big Trees', for Pureora is a forest, as it has been ever since new soils formed on a landscape reshaped by the volcanic eruptions of the central North Island and left all stirred up ready for recolonisation. To set the scene for the big sneeze, I will don the guise of a male rimu, slightly past my prime at 663 years of age.

Kokako had raised a family in a nest nearby, filling my part of the forest with their individual song. A male kiwi was still watching over its egg in a hole beneath my roots and moa were busy browsing the leaves of the tanekaha seedlings that were growing all around. Fortunately for us podocarps, these birds, both large and small, prefer to eat the soft leaves of the broad-leaf trees like false wintera, willow-leaved myrsine and, of course, northern rata.

Clever things, rata, and I should know, for a big one is growing around my trunk. Many years ago, I think it was my 501st birthday, a tiny, woody rata seed was carried up and lodged in the crotch of one of my branches. For a few years it behaved itself like a good perching plant should, and then it began to send down long, woody roots. Once they had reached the ground the rata's growth rate increased, for it was no longer dependent for water and minerals on the rain and the dust washing down my trunk. Today, part of my trunk is encased by the rata, which has put out a network of arm-like branches. The rata does me no real harm, and in a good flowering year like this one, its dark-red blossoms attract many birds to feed within our combined canopies. Being much younger than I, it will probably outlive me by many years, forming an outer living trunk while I will decay away inside. As I get more aged and infirm, the grubs and borers which feed upon my useless wood will in their turn feed many other birds and insects. It makes one feel quite important to have so many other living things depending on you, even when you have been long dead. I always hope that, when my trunk has decayed away just a little more, the bats which echo-sound their way amongst my branches by night will come to roost in my hollow trunk each day.

Bat droppings are very good organic fertiliser, and I could do with a few extra nutrients, for throughout my lifetime the soil and the forest has become impoverished. There is less *Gahnia* and kiekie growing round about today than there was in my sapling years. Perhaps they do not like the more acidic soil or the fact that the summers are a little cooler.

My ladylove is not far away through the forest, and I can see her branches burdened down with the fruits of my pollen's labours. The real problem is that there is no room in the forest for the youngsters to grow, and so we are very happy to share the fruits with the birds which carry the seeds to other parts of the forest. The great

Young rata, *Metrosideros fulgens*

Trunk of a rimu, *Dacrydium cupressinum*,
with mature vine of rata.

forest of Pureora stretches away as far as my top shoots can see, over the distant hills, an unbroken canopy of living green, so their journey may well be in vain. Oh well, that is the way of the forest.

Suddenly, way in the distance, something happens. Over in the direction in which the sun rises every day, an enormous cloud of smoke — no, it looks more solid than that — has spouted up into the sky, scattering even the highest clouds. The whole forest has become silent, as if waiting for catastrophe, and even the largest flame-of-the-forest weevils stop feeding on my wood. Then a roaring bang, much louder than any thunderclap I've ever heard, breaks the silence, as in the distance we see smoke, lit by an incandescent glare, dim the sun. A rushing, hissing wall of dust appears over the eastern ridge of the hills and rushes downslope towards us. The birds have already taken flight towards the safety of the west, and the moa and kiwi rush round in confusion, but nothing is safe, there is no place to hide. Some enormous force fells me to the ground. I am engulfed in warm, white dust and that is all I can remember until much, much later.

The next thing I can recall was a strange noise, the like of which I have never heard in the ancient forest, and again I saw the light of day, 1,800 years after I was knocked flat. Fantastic! And I can report that there is life in the old carcase yet, for already the spores of a bird's nest fungus, blown in from the new forest hereabouts, have germinated and started to make use of my wood. Also, groups of some strange animal, the like of which I have never seen, each with brightly coloured plumage, come with what I take to be adults, to look at me and scratch my likeness on flat white sheets.

Fantasy? Of course it is. Trees and forests cannot talk, but in the hands of scientists the evidence they leave behind communicates loud and clear.

The two loud noises in my story are the historic explosion of the Taupo eruption of around AD 186, which knocked the trees down although its source was fifty kilometres away, and the modern noise of a mechanical digger used to drain the swamp which had developed, preserving the remains of the forest. The strange modern animals are groups of children with a teacher or ranger. The rest is thanks to all the painstaking work carried out on the remains of the now world-famous Pureora buried forest, which is a flattened forest, with the vast majority of the trunks aligned with their root plates in the direction of Taupo. The trees are all perfectly preserved beneath a thin deposit of Taupo ignimbrite which became water-logged, for the ashfall dammed the local valley, ponding the waters back upstream. The buried forest was discovered in the autumn of 1983 by a contractor who was endeavouring to drain a series of wetlands near Pureora so that they could be planted with pines.

The ancient logs were about a metre below the surface, and the fact that very few show any sign of charring tells us that, by the time the wall of pumice arrived on the scene, it had cooled sufficiently so that this part of the great forest was not consumed by fire. All forests nearer the eruption must have been burned to a crisp or cooked to charcoal.

Detailed work has shown that at least forty-five species of plants, including twenty-six trees and shrubs, three climbers and scramblers, nine ferns, two tree

A buried botanist in the buried forest at Pureora.

Bracket fungus.

ferns and five grasses and sedges were growing in the forest. Also, there were the remains of two sorts of giant weevils, neither of which are found living anywhere on the mainland today but which were doing well back in the year 186.

The work has also allowed an assessment of the structure and make-up of the original forest. Celery-leaved pine was the dominant tree and, although all the five main podocarps were present, kahikatea was a rarity. Also, the make-up of the forest was typical of old forest soils, poor in nutrients. The presence of *Gahnia* and kiekie, which are today only found in warmer situations, to the north or at lower altitudes, indicated that they became established during the climatic optimum when temperatures were about 5°C warmer than they are today. They may well have been on their last roots in the forest at the time of the cataclysm.

Study of the remnants of the contemporary forest that are still growing amongst the monotony of the pine plantations around Pureora allow comparison of the make-up of the burned forest with those still growing today. Kiekie and *Gahnia* never made it back, though, who knows, they may still return if the world's greenhouse is getting warmer. However, much in the modern forest, which is dominated by magnificent matai and tawa, tells us that it has developed on younger, richer soils, formed from, or at least enriched by, the pumice. Tawa and the other broad-leaved trees, like kamahi and mahoe, do not thrive on nutrient-poor, acid podsols and they are now abundant in Pureora. The giant weevils, which can grow to three and a half centimetres in length, probably did return to Pureora after the eruption but have since been wiped out by the recent introduction of rats to their mainland home.

Although there were no people living on Moa's Ark 1,800 years ago, the eruption was recorded by writers in both the Roman and Chinese Empires as years of blood-red sunsets, so great was the spread of Taupo's dust. The first settlers did not arrive on the Ark for about another 900 years, by which time all the non-waterlogged soils between Pureora and Taupo were again decked with trees.

Recolonisation was probably a very rapid process, for pockets of forest must have survived in the lee of hills and ridges beyond the main zone of incineration, held in trust for the natural regeneration of the forest. Certainly the moa, kiwi and all the other birds returned, for they are recorded in the songs and legends of the tangata whenua. Tihei mauriora. Taupo's eruption surely did breathe the stuff of life into the surrounding land.

Waipapa Ecological Area, Pureora Forest.
D. WILLIAMS, FRI

PART THREE

Raiders of the Last Ark

◀ Not a native in sight — the exotic landscape of the Canterbury Plains.

WINDOW 21

Shag Bay Barbecue

It was one of those perfect days as the crew drove out to a rendezvous with pre-history down through the Shag River window. We parked on the salt marsh and waded the creek on a falling tide. In the distance, and partly hidden by the dunes, was a mirage of tents that housed a group of archaeologists. No one was home save the cook. This was the last day of the dig and we had arrived just in time to glean the fruits of their summer's labour.

The actual scene of the excavation was straight from *Raiders of the Lost Ark*, all dust, hot sun and bronzed, hardworking bodies. Instead of Harrison Ford, Atholl Anderson greeted us and led us back to the treasures of Moa's Ark. The main pit had been dug into one of the sand-dune ridges which separated the sea from the salt flats of the estuary. Everywhere, small teams of dusty excavators were working away at different levels, reaching back into the past with an assortment of tableware, artists' requisites, surgical instruments and infinite patience. Each find, be it a fragment of eggshell, a finely crafted bone fish-hook or a stone butchering knife, was put on record, accurately located in context by depth and in relation to a string grid pegged out around the edge of the hole.

Buckets of sand were raised to the surface and systematically sifted through an inclined fine-mesh sieve, the dust of prehistory blowing away downwind. Then the larger lumps were spread out in trays for a final going-over by keen eyes and deft fingers. The sorting was carried out in a small enclosure fenced on all sides with fine black netting to provide some shade from the sun and shelter from the wind. The unwanted dross was thrown up and over the netting, where it formed a new midden, an embryo dune for the future.

A cry of triumph from the centre of the pit signalled the discovery of a large artefact. Itchy fingers wanted it dragged out into the light of twentieth-century technology, but even the magic squeeze of cameraman Lemmon had to wait as brushes flicked the sand away, revealing the sternum of a large moa.

The ancestors of these giant birds had probably arrived upon the Ark by air or foot some seventy million years ago and, finding no competition for food or space, had taken command. Radiating out through time and all available space, they had seized every browsing opportunity in a land always partly covered with forest.

Great trials and tribulations came their way: the marine transgressions, when sea covered much of the Ark's eroded hulk; the great ice ages, when water in the form of ice did much the same in the South Island; not to mention a whole epidemic of big sneeze eruptions in the North Island. Early in their history, sixty-five million years ago, they had survived the Great Extinction, which snuffed out so many groups of animals, including the largest of the large land, sea and air reptiles. Even the

Digging for history with Atholl Anderson.

smallest of the small floating marine plants and animal plankton died out, and the latter are recorded in infinite detail in rocks in Shag River, where many lines of ascent of both foraminifers and coccoliths came to an abrupt halt. Just along the coast, at Moeraki Bluff, the whole story of extinction is wrapped up in giant cannon-ball concretions. The bones of mosasaurs and plesiosaurs and shells of ammonites and belemnites are found in abundance in these strange conglomerates. So it was that the way was opened up to all the survivors, amongst which were the ancestors of the moa.

Soon it was my turn to descend barefoot into the recesses of the excavation. The blackened sand was too hot for my untrained feet, and hopping about only made it worse, bringing cascades of even hotter sand falling from above. Once down and out of reach of the onshore wind, it was even more stifling, like descending into a giant oven, and that is exactly what was revealed before my dusty eyes: a series of pit ovens, one above the other, each of which had roasted moa for the local menu.

The compacted sand which marked each hearth was sintered pink by the intense heat of the roast. Above, layers of blackened sand, the remains of the wood fuel complete with tell-tale pieces of bone, set the scene. You could almost hear the fat dripping from giant capons, sizzling on the hearth, elbow-licking good and ready for the table. Equally revealing were the butchering sites and waste dumps, or middens, each telling the same story — profligate use of a key resource.

Leg bone of the largest moa, *Dinornis giganteus*.

A similar picture has emerged from every site so far excavated, the vast majority of which are situated, like Shag Point, at the mouth of a river twixt estuary and sea. A perfect place to live, for when the moa became scarce, the riches of the sea were at hand to supplement the diet.

Moa of all eleven-plus species were captured with ease, speared, clubbed to death or their necks simply wrung. Only the best cuts of the bird were taken, the rest left to rot, preserved in peat and clay to tell the tale. The thirty-minute egg must have figured large upon the menu and, fry as you may, there was no sunny side up for the dwindling population of birds.

Thanks to well-preserved crop contents, we know that the great birds were not lawn-mowers, but browsed twigs and leaves from trees and shrubs. Their dimensions tell us that, on tiptoe, the largest could reach up to more than three metres, and their gizzard stones, which are always of local provenance, indicate some form of territoriality or, at least, argue against migration. As to their fecundity, we can only guess. Ostriches, emus and rheas all lay large clutches, but are birds of open country with mammals as their neighbours, and so their nests are subject to predation. Cassowaries are forest-browsers and lay three to six eggs. Takahe lay three and kiwis usually one egg. We are therefore going to have to carry on guessing until a moa's nest is found, preserved, complete with eggs. The likelihood of finding an undisturbed nest is slim, for the eggs were used by the first humans to carry water and were valuable possessions. Even then we won't be sure, for, like the ostrich, moa may have been gregarious nesters. Whatever the answer, the artefacts that are being unearthed all the time point to predation by people as a major factor in the extinction of the moa.

Sitting high above the Shag River, it is easy to understand how the story of a great canoe bringing the ancestors of the local tribe to this perfect spot has been preserved. There it is, carved in stone complete with helmsman standing in the stern, but wrecked on the beach. Just around the corner, those cannonball conglomerations could be the abandoned luggage.

An armada of migrants or a series of lone canoes drifting helplessly off course? The enigma of the Maori discovery of Aotearoa still waits to be unravelled. The shortest open-sea journey from their erstwhile home in the South Pacific is at least 3,000 kilometres, so, either way, it was a magnificent act of seamanship and survival.

Did the early Polynesian migrants bring their tropical crops — kumara, taro, gourd and paper mulberry — and the Polynesian dog and rat with them? Or did they make return voyages to stock up at some later date? The latter would appear quite likely, for the kumara, which is of South American origin, did not arrive in Polynesia until more recent times. Equally puzzling is their rapid conversion from tropical horticulture, which had sustained their ancestors for hundreds if not thousands of years, to subtropical and even temperate hunting and gathering, a totally new way of life at which they evidently excelled. People arrived on Moa's Ark about a thousand years ago and took to the smorgasbord lifestyle. Exploring the coastline took a mere generation, but penetration inland took a little longer. Five hundred years after the first landings, the moa population was heading for extinction.

When Europeans first arrived on the scene, they found much of the eastern half of the South Island covered with tussock grassland, right down to sea level. A semi-arid climate and the hot dry winds blowing across the bare mountain flanks were the obvious explanation for the lack of forest. The presence of charred tree stumps in amongst the tussock was more difficult to explain, as were the enormous forests, some still standing but buried under great depths of river gravel and shingle in excavations under the Canterbury Plains. Natural fire, over a very long period of time, was blamed, the erosion of the mountain slopes so caused inundating the coastal forests. But radiocarbon dating put most of the stumps at less than a thousand years, placing the time of destruction well and truly in the Maori fire period. Fires for cooking, fires for clearing land, fires running out of control. There is now little doubt but that the Maori hunters, ably assisted by two other introduced mammals, kuri (the Polynesian dog) and kiore (the Polynesian rat), as well as fire, destroyed as much as half the native forests and pushed the moa to the very edge of extinction.

To seek a simple explanation as to why the forests did not regenerate after fire is like looking for a wishbone in a moa oven — they did not have one, and there probably isn't one. Repeated fire, coarse gravel and black, swelling, clay-based soils are some reasons, but the overriding non-availability of moisture, or soil-water deficit, is probably the main culprit. Any soil that loses 200 millimetres of water more than it gains in an average year poses a problem to the regeneration of New Zealand's native trees. A soil-water deficit of 300 millimetres appears to preclude forest regeneration, and that's the way it was, and sometimes is, east of the Southern Alps.

Kaimaumau Swamp — ravaged by fire.

Oparara R.I.P.

If it had just been the moa that disappeared, the world would have mourned their loss but the voyage of their Ark would not have been in vain. The list of onboard extinctions is, however, both long and diverse — and it does not stop in Maori times. The threat still hangs over many beautiful and important plants and animals even today.

The contemporary problems are matters of day-to-day concern, debate and media report, but how do we know what had disappeared before the advent of written history? To find out, we must step back through a time window carved in rock by running water.

At the southern end of the Heaphy Track, one of the great bush walks of New Zealand, and at the northern end of the Queenstown–Westport–Karamea road (which shows an increasing number of tourists one of the least-spoilt coastlines in the world), just past Karamea, there sits a lump of rock. Well, you could call it rock, for the Oparara Block is made of limestone and it is certainly a lump of about one square kilometre, but it is more like Gruyère cheese, full of holes and the flavour of a pure organic past.

We rose early to find the gale-force winds and torrential rain of the past few days had stopped, and went along to the Department of Conservation's local headquarters to be kitted out for caving. Hard hats, acetylene lamps, nylon boilersuits and guides. The first leg of the journey by four-wheel-drive hit problems in the shape of washouts and tracks covered with fallen trees and mudslides: the rain had done its worst. A mechanical digger was called to the rescue and we followed it up to base camp, a hut in the middle of what had been natural rainforest, now desecrated with gums. Don't get me wrong, I am not against eucalypts when planted in the right place, but karst country close to one of the true wonders of the natural world is not the right place.

Gear on, we walked down well-kept paths towards the Oparara Block and at each turn of the track savoured a taste of what lay in store. Everywhere, native forest dripped with filmy ferns; liverworts, mosses and lichens clung to trunks and cliffs alike, hiding the jumble of water-worn karst country.

Karst landscapes are some of the strangest and most beautiful in the world, each one created through time by heavy rainfall on limestone. The willow-pattern rockscapes of China, the Plitvice Lakes of Yugoslavia and the Knife Pinnacles of the Gunung Mulu in Sarawak are all karst-country national parks and World Heritage sites. Oparara still waits for international acclaim.

A clump of Prince of Wales feather fern waved in the stillness of the forest; the trees were stirred by a strong breeze coming up through a small vent — one of the

Leaving the world of the present — the entrance to Oparara Caves.

multitude of exits and entrances, depending on your size, into the cave systems below. A gaping chasm, framed in green as natural as nature meant it to be, except for a path and steps designed to minimise visitor damage, led us down into the rock. There beside the path was the first tangible evidence of extinction, the remains of a moa, part-hidden by a fall of rock, and then another and another. 'Lights on now,' we were instructed as we made our way down into inky blackness. Looking back, we saw an oval void framed in black, the last sight for many birds as they made their way down into the halls of doom. The distant warmth of the sun called us back, but the excitement of discovery and the hiss of carbide and water drew us on around the first tight corner.

The Department of Conservation has done a magnificent job: the path guides but in no way intrudes upon the spirit of the place, and to date there has been no need to vandal-proof even the most delicate of cave formations. Stalactites and -mites (the latter go up), fine veils of travertine, straws leaning in the wind, cave deposits, muds and silts on floors, sides and cuttings undisturbed for millennia are there to see, and, everywhere, little heaps of bones — weka, kokako, kakapo, wrens — each one telling the same sad story: the end of one life, the beginning of others. For, though the bones were there intact, the flesh and feathers have gone, eaten away by insects, fungi and bacteria. Lights off, and as human eyes accommodated to the gloom, the lights of thousands of glow-worms lit the void above, specks of bright-green phosphorescence set against a semi-twilight. Daylight not far ahead, suffusing through the labyrinth, allowed just a smidgeon of green growth on the wetter rocks.

As we turned yet another corner, the sun struck midday and streamed almost vertically down through one of the highlights of Oparara: a giant cleft or crack, known as a tomo, funnelling up to the sky. An eye on heaven, complete with lashes of tree ferns and vines, leaning in as if distorted by a fish-eye lens: with the added surprise of an eye full of water drops, iridescent tears cascading from above, unsalted sympathy for the little heaps of bones which lay all about. The saddest of all being those of a kakapo, which some time in the not too dim and distant past must have tumbled or wandered into the cave system and, finding no food and no way out, lay down to die in a dry corner near those tantalising rays of hope, its final death kick wedging its clawed feet beneath a shelf of rock.

Our way led on, ever upwards through the system, ascending the stream, knee-deep in places, through cataracts and waterfalls, along ledges and side channels long abandoned by the water that had carved and polished their walls. All the time we kept to marked tracks in order to minimise damage to the cave deposits, which tell of currents, climates and environments long past, and hide the remains of birds still waiting to be discovered.

The roof of the chamber sloped down to meet our now-stooping forms, bringing a twinge of danger. Why were there so many skeletons scattered on the ground? What dreadful secret did these inner recesses of Moa's Ark hold in store? Lights splashed across the roof and dozens of exoskeletons withdrew into deep cracks. Nothing to fear, only cave wetas on the prowl. But, there, a larger flatter shape, eight legs, six centimetres across, large enough to make even an arachnophile jump. *Grandungula*, the great black spider. Apologies, it has had its name changed to *Spelungula*, for it lives only in caves, where it feeds on insects all much smaller than the smallest speleologist.

We turned off our lights and waited for the wetas to regroup, and as we did, the void all around was lit up by glow-worm lights. The cave of hidden terror became a cathedral lit by the adaptive radiation of the insects. Cave glow-worms are a sort of midge which, in its adult form, flies and mates upon the wing. The female then lays her eggs safe in a cave or beneath an overhang, where, like those of all insects, they hatch and then pass through a series of larval stages called instars. The glow-worms spin a transparent tube within which each instar lives up to its name. This illuminating tale does not stop there, for each larva also dangles a fishing line, a chandelier complete with lustres of stickum which reflect the light, luring and ensnaring the prey. Each cave is thus a way of life, a place of safety for its own and a place of death for intruders from above.

The skeleton of a kiore was there to prove that they too had invaded even these deep recesses of the Ark. Kiore are omnivores, but feed mainly on grass seeds and the like. They may well have picked the last meat off the bones in desperation, but they could never have dispatched the big birds. So what had been the cause of all these deaths?

The answer is very prosaic and perhaps difficult to believe. It is entirely natural; natural accident and death. Like humans, all animals are prone to accidents and all

The mid-day sun lights up the hidden world of Oparara.

Moa bones.
ROD MORRIS

become aged and infirm. Birds, especially if they were poor fliers or flightless, could wander or fall into the caves and, unable to make their way out, would die of starvation. Likewise, very old individuals might seek shelter from the rain within the caves and die and their bones would rest in peace. We know there are not, and never have been, any wolves, foxes, bears, cats or dogs, no mammals to desecrate their resting place.

Plausible? Yes, but why are there so many skeletons in Oparara's cupboard. Well, one accident or death each year for twenty thousand years makes twenty thousand piles of bones. The rate of accident and natural death in one square kilometre of karst must be much higher than that, and the caves have been there much longer than twenty thousand years. Oparara is a showcase of the past inhabitants of Moa's Ark.

Our final act of homage to this very special place was when we were allowed to crawl on hands and knees into another cave in which amazing discoveries have been made. The entrance is guarded by grilles and gates and padlocks, for a new breed of grave-robber is at large. It is a sad fact of modern life that the treasures within must be given full protection. We moved in single file between two orange tapes laid out on the floor to guide us on our way, the roof so low at one point we had to crawl flat on our bellies. Our reptilian crawling gait moved our headlamp beams from side to side, raking over bones strewn in every direction. They protruded from an octagonal crackwork of dried cave alluvium and were partly covered with the dust of time which had filtered down into this place. This was the final resting place of no fewer than forty-two moa, their remains washed in while this particular cave was still in contact with the living water that has carved them all.

Lying in the dark, flat on my back, waiting for the lights to go on and filming to commence, the press of catastrophe was all around. What if there was an earthquake and this time slot in the rock collapsed? The frail imprints of our presence would be there together with those of the moa.

144

The remains of glories past speak to us, for in these and other cave systems across New Zealand we can find a record of those other bird species that joined at least eleven species of moa on the roll call of the extinct.

R.I.P. (the Rest In sPecies)

New Zealand pelican *Pelecanus novaezelandiae*
Flightless goose *Cnemiornis calcitrans*
New Zealand swan *Cygnus sumnerensis*
Finsch's duck *Euryanas finschi*
New Zealand hawk *Circus eylesi*
Haast's eagle *Harpagornis moorei*
New Zealand quail *Coturnix novaezelandiae*
Snipe-rail *Capellirallus karamu*
New Zealand giant coot *Fulica chathamensis chathamensis*
Chatham Island rail *Gallirallus modestus*
Hodgen's waterhen *Gallinula hodgenorum*
Dieffenbach's rail *Gallirallus philippensis dieffenbachi*
Adze bill *Aptornis otidiformis*
Chatham Island snipe *Coenocorypha chathamica*
Giant owlet-nightjar *Aegotheles eristatus*
New Zealand raven *Corvus moriorum*
Stephens Island wren *Traversia lyalli*
Stout-legged wrens *Pachyplichas yaldwini* and *Pachyplichas jagmi*
Piopio *Turnagra capensis*
Huia *Heteralocha acutirostris*

It may be that the laughing owl, *Sceloglaux albifacies*, and the bush wren, *Xenicus longipes*, still survive tucked away in some forest recesses of the South Island. They must be getting very lonely now, and the likelihood is that these two species are also gone forever.

WINDOW 23

The Aupouri Tombolo

The subtropical climate of the far north of the North Island attracts discerning holidaymakers like a magnet. Up and away from the nightlife hustle of Auckland, past the lure of coloured canvas and the power of boats in the Bay of Islands, through deserted degraded kaurilands to the peace and ruffled calm of the Aupouri Tombolo — a long finger of partly mobile sand which points either scorn at past practices of land abuse or hope at sustainable use in the future. This peninsula is dotted with magic names.

Ninety Mile Beach, clean sand washed by purest sea, perfect but for those who race its length in two- and four-wheel-drive vehicles. The peace of wilderness, a quality of life, a human right, must it be a thing of the past?

Parengarenga Harbour, a maze of amazing tidal waters, possibly the purest and most unpolluted on the earth, home to a wealth of fish and shellfish, of seabirds and the people of the Muriwhenua. The Surville Cliffs, the prow of Moa's Ark, one tip of the tail of Maui's Fish, are made of serpentine, a natural rock which contains such a wealth of chemicals toxic to plants — magnesium, nickel, chromium and cobalt. Spiced with onshore salt-laden tropical winds, the soil cannot support the growth of large trees. Plants, however, are in plenty, but they have their own endemic character and characteristics.

Cape Reinga, and the pohutukawa tree that never celebrated Christmas, for it has never flowered. This is a most sacred Maori place, where the spirits of the people take leave of their homeland and pass to their spiritual home through the sea and the Three Kings Islands, some sixty kilometres further north by west.

Great Island, in the Three Kings group, where the rarest plant in the world, *Tecomanthe speciosa*, took its last stand, waiting for extinction. There was, indeed, just one plant left growing out of the way of even the most adventurous goat, when conservation and horticulture gave a hand and saved it for another day. Now there are many thousands of plants in cultivation, gracing gardens and greenhouses, ready for re-introduction.

Tecomanthe is one of six plants endemic to the Three Kings and of oriental (well, at least of tropical) origin. Another five endemics are also found on the islands, but these have their origins in more southerly subtropical and temperate New Zealand. This is in marked contrast to the flora of the North Cape, whose forests are poor, both in endemics and in plants of tropical affinity. The explanation is, in all probability, that during the ice ages, cooler conditions and a more temperate vegetation pushing up from the south edged tropical plants out of the mainland. The Three Kings, isolated by warm sea water, were not so badly affected and thus the tropical elements hung on.

The prow of Moa's Ark — rock formations at North Cape.

Parengarenga Harbour, the northernmost estuary in Northland.

One other reason for extinction and impoverishment of the mainland flora lies in the fact that the tombolo is mostly sand dunes, linking and partly overriding a series of rocky islands. The vast bulk of this sandspit, which is more than 100 kilometres long, is less than 100,000 years old. The recent history of the place appears to involve a number of phases of sand stabilisation by forest, including kauri and podocarps, interspersed with periods of dune mobility. Here is another explanation of the enigma of kauri forest regeneration. Ancient trees, suppressing their young, eventually lose their grip on the sand, which blows, destroys, rejuvenates and is once more stabilised by forest. The latest phase of stabilisation appears to have begun some 5,000 years ago.

When the ancestors of the Te Aupouri people arrived on the tombolo, they made large stone adzes which would have been used for felling and working wood and for digging. The scratches on the adzes prove they were not idle, and the evidence dates back 700 years.

The tombolo is (or was, before massive plantation of pine for sand stabilisation) a unique place for the study of middens, encampments and settlements. Among the mobile dunes there is no need to dig excavations: all the archaeologist needs is patience; the wind will do the rest. Two main groups of sites have been identified amongst the many hundreds which have been revealed by the shifting sands of recent time. A dense belt of coastal sites remains, no more than 300 metres inland from the dune front, and a scattering of sites between one and five kilometres inland.

The rubbish in the middens of the inland sites tells us that the people were, in the main, nomadic gatherers, making use of the rich beds of shellfish from both

Houhora midden, a rubbish dump full of prehistory.

148

coasts, which are nowhere far apart. They collected toheroa and tuatua from the length of Ninety Mile Beach, mudsnails, pipi and cockles from the still waters of the harbours, and mussels and cat's-eyes from the rocky eastern shores. Fish were not an important part of their diet — perhaps the waters of the unprotected coast were too rough, although snapper bones show they fished the harbours. They were not bird-eaters, and the presence of whale bone shows that cetaceans have always become stranded on the beaches hereabouts.

The coastal sites are of great interest, for there is no sign of long-term occupation. The smallest middens may represent no more than a barbecue stop along Ninety Mile Beach, while the largest, which are really large and contain up to eighty tonnes of crushed and burned shells, suggest a completely different activity. Could they be industrial waste from the large-scale production of dried shellfish for inland home consumption, or even for barter? Coromandel basalt, argillite from Nelson and obsidian from Mayor Island, almost 400 kilometres away by sea, show that the people were not stay-at-homes.

The presence of land-snail shells in the middens is of great interest, as is their discovery in subfossil form *in situ* in the dunes. All point to the presence of coastal scrub and broad-leaf forest covering the dunes in the not too far distant past.

The story derived from these sites, as from many other middens, is much the same. The first settlers came and made use of everything their local landscape hypermart had on offer. Moa, goose, rail, seabirds that nested on land, seals, penguins, fish, crayfish, shellfish; the riches of the land and sea. The Maori adapted their lifestyles and developed new technologies of survival.

Certain middens show the whole picture in intricate layered detail: moa eaten until no more, likewise seals and seabirds, shells and carapaces, large at first, become smaller and smaller with time, until at last, the resource depleted, the locals must move on to richer pickings or pick a fight with their neighbours.

The lucky ones, especially in the warm subtropic north, fell back on their ancestral horticulture; perhaps — who knows when or how — returning to their homeland to bring back crop plants like kumara, taro and gourd. Even if they had carried that genetic stock with them in the first place, and maintained it in cultivation throughout their time of smorgasbord exploration, the Maori gardeners had to develop new skills. North Cape is not the tropics, and Moa's Ark still had to ride out the Little Ice Age, which raked the seventeenth-century world, ruining crops and starving millions of people.

The growth of crops, especially out of their natural environmental range, depends first and foremost on the selection of the right genetic strains. All crop plants started their life as wild weeds which attracted the gastronomic attention of people gathering a livelihood from native bush. Most wild plants show a good deal of genetic variation and thrive across a range of environments. Kumara is a good example. It originated in South America, and selection from the original genestock allowed cultivars to be grown across an enormous range of altitudes, from the dry and humid tropics to the heights of the Andes. Part of this variety was taken to Polynesia and on to New Zealand. The same is true for the taro, which had its origins in South-East Asia.

Taro cultivation needs swamps, and New Zealand abounded with such wet, undrained places which, with a little bit of taming, could be made productive. What is more, taro and, especially the first flush of wonderfully nutritious leaves, grows very quickly in the warmth of summer.

Kumara is more difficult, but there were north-facing slopes warmed by the sun: fields were cleared and the stones removed and piled into shelter strips. Ridge and furrow were laboriously dug to draw away the cold soil water, and raised plots were made with blackened stone to catch and hold the heat of the sun, a little bit of tropical magic to sweeten the potato and the lifestyle. Changing times, changing ways. So it was that, about 500 years after they had arrived on Aotearoa, those Maori people lucky enough to live in the warm north were able to rekindle ancient practices, break new ground and grow old crops. It was in the breaking of this new ground that still more forest cover was removed from the land, ushering in a new phase of erosion across the dunes of the Aupouri Tombolo and the other, more friable soils of Moa's Ark.

Before taking leave of this game of life played out on the tombolo of sand and rock, there are two living museums that are worth much more than a passing mention.

The first are the Surville Cliffs, made of serpentine and rising sheer out of a subtropic sea. On one of the most northerly of the bluffs there is a rock jutting out high over the waves creaming around the forefoot of Moa's Ark. A fitting figure-head, for it is shaped like a giant tuatara, Old Beak Head himself, carrying the gathered wisdom of the ages on into an uncertain future.

There, amongst those tortured rocks and strong enough to ride out the storms of time, is the most bizarre collection of plants to be found anywhere in New Zealand. Mature celery-top pines, pohutukawa and many other trees grow no taller than a child. A subtropic bonsai world in which plant growth is held down by a mixture of exposure, toxic chemicals and, in the summer, long periods of drought and intense heat at rock level. Everywhere, the parasitic tropical dodder grows in bright yellow-orange mats, feeding from the trees and shrubs; and, strangest of all, many shrubs appear to have given up the upward struggle and have taken on a semi-lianoid habit of growth. They produce long trailing stems, sort of feelers, which sprangle across the cliffs. Sprangling is a cross between sprawling and dangling, and wherever it takes their fancy and the soil comes close enough, the stems put down roots. Of the 144 native vascular (or higher) plants recorded from the cliffs, most appear stunted or modified in some way, and tests have shown that some of these ground-hugging traits are genetically determined. No less than fifteen of the plants are local endemics.

How, then, have they managed to survive in this tiny northern outpost, when so much of the country around about has been subjected to massive change in recent years? There is every indication that the fires which sweep across so much of the North Cape rarely, if ever, run over and down the many faces of the Surville Cliffs; the updraughts of air blowing in from the sea would always fan them the other way. So it is that the prow of the Ark is a very special refugium for genetic information relating to life in a harsh toxic environment, a museum of the past, a gene bank for

Sprangling stem of windswept manuka, *Leptospermum scoparium.*

the future. A gene bank within the repositories of which the flax snail, one of the rarest snails in the world, lives in peace.

The second museum is much easier to visit. It is the tourist stop at Houhora, bearing the name of Wagener, and it leads us on through the corridors of changing time. Not so much a museum, more a way of life, it engulfs you with ephemera of all our recent pasts. It is a wonderful collage of a place overflowing with information, the only museum I know with two burned-out pianos. The ginger squares in the café are great eating. At the back of the museum, the contents of which overflow across the grass, there is a golf course, built partly on an ancient midden. In the early days of this idyllic course the local birdie was the moa, the eagle *Harpagornis*, and the pa was just over there.

The Snares

To gain a glimpse of paradise, the paradise that existed upon Moa's Ark before the raiders came that way, we travelled south to the Snares, a group of sub-Antarctic Islands.

We knew we were in for a rough trip, the friendly voice of the weather forecaster had told us so. Invercargill basked in sun and the tinsel-studded Christmas street decorations looked well and truly out of place. The Department of Conservation's good ship *Renown* had made it through mountainous seas from patrol in the calm waters of Fiordland, and we set sail from Bluff into a glorious blustery afternoon. The trip was a cross between horizontal bungi-jumping and forced feeding, but amazingly, none of the camera crew, all of whom were seasick, had severe mishaps. I was lucky. After a hearty meal of mutton sandwiches washed down with ale, the next thing I knew was waking up to the good news that the Snares were on both the radar and the port beam. We steamed into safe anchorage in dead calm water all set about with rocks, ate breakfast (those who could face it) and so began one of the most perfect days I have ever spent anywhere upon this earth.

The sea around and beneath us was as clear as gin, so clear that we could see our anchor twenty-five metres away upon the bottom. Land lines were rigged fore and aft, each one travelling for part of its length beneath the surface of the sea, a strict precaution to prevent rats from passing from ship to shore.

Fur seals basked in the sun and sea lions played among the bull kelp, sending the penguins shooting out of the water as fast as fins and flippers could propel them. Both these marine mammals, which make the Snares their home, are members of the same group. They have external ears and move on land by turning their back flippers forward and hopping — they are both very agile on the flat and show a remarkable turn of speed. The sea lions have elastic ribs, shock absorbers affording protection when they are bashed about in the waves. These are not the performing sea lions so often seen in circuses, which are a different species originating from California. Hooker's sea lion, the local act, is only found on the Snares, Auckland and Campbell Islands. The penguins, too, are very special, being the Snares Island crested variety: 100,000-plus of them nest here and nowhere else.

A welcoming party, formally dressed in black and white tails, came out to greet us as we landed in the bay. They showed no real fear and had certainly forgotten the habits of the sealers who found rich pickings here in the past. The only thing they would not let you do was stroke their stubby feathers.

Two almost continuous streams of penguins were making their way across the shore: one heading out to sea, rejoicing in the coolness of the water after a long hot waddle, the others returning from a fishing trip. Slightly plumper and finding the hot

Bull kelp, *Durvillea antarctica*, at low tide.

The big no-no! Mooring lines could bring rodents onto the Snares.
KIM WESTERSKOV

weather somewhat inclement, they made their way up into the shade of the forest — and what a forest! Although growing in great luxuriance, it is nowhere more than ten metres tall and most of it much lower. Its canopy is made up of only two trees, both members of the daisy flower family, an olearia and a ragwort. A white-flowered, sweet-scented hebe added a little diversity, but only near the forest margins.

It is easy to be a botanist on the Snares, for the flora of trees, shrubs, herbs and ferns totals only twenty-four species. The same goes for the field of terrestrial zoology, for, coincidentally, there are twenty-four bird species and visiting marine mammals. As for marine biology, well, we will leave that for the next film, for the sea abounds with a diversity of life below the bull kelp fringe.

Having gained the full confidence of the shoreward party, we followed them up the beach and into the forest, deviating around each parked fur seal and giving the sea lions a much wider berth. The Department of Conservation maintains a long wooden walkway set on stilts to guide visitors inland, so minimising potential damage to the highly organic peaty soils. It was from this timber-top vantage point that we filmed up into the canopy of daisies and down onto the marching penguins. Their highways and byways are well marked, for millions of neat webbed feet, which look as if they are wearing spats made of pink baize, have passed this way over the centuries. In some situations, the outward-bound mums and dads (they take it in turns) would take the high road, while the incomers chose the low, while in other places the contraflow waddlers used the same stretch, bowing and nodding to each

Bull kelp, a fur seal and Snares crested penguins, *Eudyptes robustus*.
ROD MORRIS

other as they went their separate ways. At one point, where there were two very distinct ways up and down, the penguins appeared to stop and make a rational choice. One route required a not-inconsiderable jump, which all the downhillers took, skidding in the wet peat as they landed. Some of the uphill mob took the risk, most making it, but some sliding back and ruining the whiteness of their attire. Others, after due consideration, took the other route, around one of the legs of the aerial walkway. Over the years this leg has wobbled under the weight of passing scientists, eroding a spiral hole in the deep peat. Those penguins who were not too portly could use it as a spiral walkway, shuffling their way up to the top and, except for the fattest, keeping their waistcoats clean.

At the end of the walkway we all found out just how difficult intra-island travel is on the Snares: perhaps that is how they got their name — snares everywhere. If only we were penguin-size.

The semi-upright branches of the two bushy trees had to be navigated with great care, and daisy wood is very hard on the head and the shins. It was like crawling through a three-dimensional maze. Whoever invented camera tripods? To make it worse, the ground beneath your feet was very soft and riddled with nest holes of diving prions and muttonbirds. What is more, most of them were occupied by one of the parents, busy looking after the next generation of tunnellers. It was like walking across a sponge cake that had been well eaten by mice. One false step and you not only lost your footing but also your conservation badge. Progress was painfully slow, and everywhere in the distance we could see the penguin hordes wending their ancient ways up and down. Eventually we made it up to the top of the island, where one group of happy penguins were being reunited with much display and regurgitation of the fish catch.

Filming all the way back down, we were unsafe in the knowledge that we were going to have to make that same trip at least three more times, and in the dark. Mission impossible, but well worth the effort to record one of the wonders of this living world.

Evening came via a spectacular sunset as we kitted up and checked cameras, batteries and lamps. The clear sky glowed a light blue-black and a gathering wind rustled the branches of the olearia. As we walked and crawled upwards again, specks began to gather in the void above, easing themselves through soft focus into reality: the vanguard of twelve million muttonbirds, half of whom were intent on coming in to join their mates in the burrows. Above the gaunt outlines of the daisy trees, another living, wheeling, calling canopy came into being. Shades of Alfred Hitchcock. Each bird rode the wind back and forth, searching the landscape for some sign to tell it just where to drop in on its mate safe underground. The rustling of soft wings and cries of recognition grew to a rumbling, then to a mighty thundering as down through the branches the birds came a-tumbling.

Flaps down, undercarriage locked, in they came, crash-landing in every direction. Muttonbirds may be excellent fliers, but once on the ground they are plain awkward. The lucky ones crashed down quite close, some right into their burrows, and retreated underground to what sounded like a not-so-certain welcome. The others, whose aim had been not quite so accurate, rushed about, scurrying from burrow to

Muttonbirds rafting at sea.
COMMUNICATE NEW ZEALAND

Sooty shearwaters, or muttonbirds, in the Snares Island forest.
ROD MORRIS

burrow, until they found the right welcoming beak. The heavy rain of muttonbirds was interspersed with volleys of grapeshot, tiny diving prions which appeared to fold up on impact and roll around the ground like a cross between an animated ping-pong ball and a collapsed shuttlecock.

Our lights did not help anyone but the cameraman. The birds did not seem to take any notice, but the rest of us were left blinking and night-blind. I sat still and composed my words.

By the time we had wended our way back down through the now pitch-black forest, across the soft spongy ground, now gurgling with billings and cooings, it was coming up to half past eleven. Three hours later we dragged ourselves from our bunks and repeated the whole tortuous journey, right up to the highest point and over to a broad, well-worn ledge high above a slope which led down to the South Pacific — the launch pad of at least half a million muttonbirds.

We sat down just below the take-off point with lights and cameras at the ready for the early-morning fly-past. It was cold and I was snoozing when all hell began to break loose, as squadrons of muttonbirds appeared from all around, scrabbling through the tussocks and grouping ready for lift-off. A quick rush downhill, primaries feathered for the take-off, and away they went. Birds who were not lucky with a gust of wind, together with those unpractised in mob formation flying, crashed in heaps upon the ground. At one time I had no less than five perched on my shoulders and head, and another eight or nine on my lap. Feeling kind, I decided to provide a launching pad, so I stood upright in the flight path of Squadron 1055: the result — guano mayhem.

The sun began to wake the world to another day as light lifted the eyelid of the sea, and still the birds came, wave upon wave, feathered formations off to the fishing grounds. It was time for our breakfast once again, the end of another twenty-four hours in paradise. Well, twelve million muttonbirds can't be wrong.

Another sub-Antarctic storm was on the brew and we had to wait until the next day to leave this place of haven. The work went on, filming and recording, more beaks, flippers, feet, ears, whiskers, teeth, flowers and fruits, wetas and scale bugs, behaviour and courtship, chase and survival, the essence and rhythm of life which had powered Moa's Ark before the advent of humans.

We finally took our leave, after our Department of Conservation guide had finished checking and resetting the rat traps, laid around each potential landing place. The news was good, no bait had been taken, no rat remains or droppings had been seen. The protective snares of Snares were empty, paradise was safe and sound for a little longer.

Captain Cook

Abel Janszoon Tasman was the first to clap European eyes on Aotearoa, and the Dutch explorers must have seen the pohutukawa in flower, for it was December 1642 when the landing party faced the wrath of the local landlords. It was not until 7 October 1769, when Nicholas Young on the *Endeavour* sighted what is now Young Nicks Head at Poverty Bay, that Europeans were recorded as having rediscovered Moa's Ark. Also in New Zealand waters during 1769 was a French ship, the *Saint Jean Baptiste*, commanded by de Surville, which made landfall in December. At one time the two vessels were only fifty nautical miles apart, neither aware of the other's presence.

When Lieutenant James Cook, captain of the *Endeavour*, set sail from his home port of Whitby on the coast of Yorkshire, he left behind low cliffs of rapidly eroding rock, one product of which was a black substance called jet which floated on the sea. Jet became both famous and valuable after the death of Prince Albert, for Queen Victoria decked herself out in black fashion jewellery which befitted a state of mourning and an empire followed suit, leaving the ribbon industry in tatters and people starving in the mill towns of England. So it was that the first jet set came into being. Whitby jet is a subfossil gum produced by the ancestors of our modern monkey-puzzle trees — conifers not unrelated to the kauri giants that exploded their cones across both Gondwana and Laurasia in an eighty-million-year-old gum salute as Moa's Ark set sail.

The first New Zealand landfall of the *Endeavour* was near present-day Gisborne, and in November Cook landed in the estuary of what came to be called the River Thames. There is a modest monument near the town of Thames to mark the spot. Twenty kilometres upriver, Joseph Banks, the ship's botanist, encountered some of the tallest, straightest trees he had ever seen, and Cook must have been both amazed and fascinated as the first kahikatea spars fell to the metal axe, to the melodious accompaniment of bellbirds, kokako and huia. Kahikatea may be straight-grained, but it is resin-free and very prone to rot, so the one small tree felled by Cook's men never lived up to its naval promise.

It seems strange that young Joseph did not climb the banks of the river to find the source of the lumps of gum that floated on its waters. It was left to the French to discover the kauri, the best hard softwood in the world, especially when it came to building boats.

It was these first discoveries which led to the raiding of the Ark and its treasures on a massive scale, and the list of European atrocities against the Maori, Maoridom and the mana of their environment do not make happy reading.

Let us get the records straight. The Maori were neither conservationists nor preservationists. They were skilled hunters and gatherers, and where the climate and the gene pool allowed, talented in horticulture — so talented that there were at least 100,000 Maori living off the waning bounty of their island home. They cultivated no fewer than seventy varieties of kumara as far south as Banks Island — well, that is what Cook called it — and taro down to, but not beyond, the suntraps of Nelson. South of this, the people still hunted the dwindling moa population and lived by snaring smaller birds, fishing the sea and rivers for eels and lampreys, gathering fruits and berries and shellfish. The digging of fern root, or rather, the underground stem of the edible bracken, was widespread, for it had become a staple part of the Maori diet, especially in those open areas of cut-over and burnt bush where it thrived, out of competition with trees.

These had been the evolving ways of Maori life since the fourteenth century — complete with the most intricate body tattoos and resource tapu in the world; woodcarving of immense proportions and exquisite execution; flax and pingao craft; and, of course, the woof and warp of civilisation, the stratagems of war. The story of Cain and Abel was re-enacted on the decks of Moa's Ark, just as it had been across the world wherever the meek had inherited the poorer soils. Those who had good land to hand, rather than the wayward promise of wild birds in the bush, grew in strength. They had homes with crops to guard and a firmer energy base from which to fight.

Time on many hands makes fighting work, and spears that once had hunted the giant birds were again unleashed on the killing fields. The songs of the people tilling soils in unison gave way to the war chants of the great canoes forging through the water and into conflict. The arts of digging kumara pits, terracing the best north-facing slopes, erecting windbreaks and excavating drainage and irrigation ditches were put to other uses. Maori engineering skills became less civil but more elaborate, as fortified pa, complete with entrenchments and revets, were carved out of tall vantage points. Pa served the Maori well in fights among themselves and against the increasing numbers of Europeans but were no defence against measles and other introduced diseases which ripped through the Maori population. In next to no time they were decimated, and by the end of the nineteenth century, war and pestilence had wiped out more than three-quarters of the Maori people.

In 1793 Philip King arrived in New Zealand from nearby New South Wales and penned the following report back to London: 'Much publik good would result to the commerce of Great Britain and these colonies if a settlement was made at the Bay of Islands or the River Thames.'

Later, when King became the Governor of New South Wales, he not only gave instructions to send pigs and crop materials to New Zealand whenever the opportunity occurred, but also entertained Te Pahi, an important chief from the Bay of Islands, for three months in Parramatta. So the export/import business was opened up, and myriad sails began to be seen around the many islands of Moa's Ark.

The year 1792 saw the first sealer gangs on shore, and more followed, raiding the mainland and the island fur-seal colonies as far south as the Snares. They clubbed the seals, they skinned them, they ate them, and to help render their fat down for export, they used penguins as fuel. At first, the trade was administered from Governor King's colony and much of the booty went to China, for the famous

Dairy cows and a remnant of kahikatea forest.

East India Company had the monopoly on the trade of furs and skin in Britain.

The Americans were soon in on the act, and one of their ships, *The Favourite*, carried off no less than 60,000 skins in one voyage, helping to seal the fate of these peaceful, doe-eyed animals. What had happened to the great birds on land over a period of more than five centuries now overtook the mammalian denizens of the sea in fifty years. Indeed, only twenty years later, in 1812, there were so few fur seals left that the hunt was abandoned, not because of conservationist zeal but for economic reasons.

Whales were next on the agenda of slaughter: the toothed sperm whales, which fed on the Pacific squid, and the southern rights, baleen whales which sieved the krill in bays and inshore waters. Not as easy as clubbing seals and, unfortunately, not as quick and humane. The whale nation were mercilessly hunted by harpoon from rowing boats. It was no mean feat; there was no time for mercy and none was shown, for bulls, pregnant cows and calves went the same slow, gory way, their great brains, filled with the accumulated wisdom of the sea, rendered down for chemicals. Soon more baleen — whalebone — was floating around the ballrooms of the British Empire than was left in the inshore waters of Moa's Ark.

Americans, and especially Puritans from New England, figured large in those years of appalling cruelty, but the traders also came from Tasmania, New South Wales, France and Holland. They sought sperm whale oil for soaps, candlewax, cosmetics and a whole host of chemicals without which the Industrial Revolution, unlubricated, would have ground to a halt.

The behaviour of both Maori and Europeans alike in the ports and shore stations which served and serviced the lust of cetaceanicide was no different from that in many ports, taverns, bordellos and boardrooms across the world at the value-added end of this sad episode of history. The senseless slaughter still drags on in the hypocrisies of so-called scientific whaling.

Stand above that small, sad, black-edged window into time, the monument to Captain Cook, and take a 360° look at the landscape. Green fields of perennial rye-grass; cows' tails often docked for mechanised convenience, poplar and apple trees, and yes, there in the distance, a lone group of kahikatea, the only native tree left. Forest clearance on an unprecedented scale was next upon the lists of European destruction, but not before a treaty between Maori and European was signed to allow matters to proceed lawfully.

160

The Bridge to Nowhere

With the signing of the Treaty of Waitangi in 1840, a new age of destruction of the resources of Moa's Ark began in earnest, with little regard to the spirit, let alone the letter, of the law. The new world of commerce was crying out not only for seal skin and whale oil, but also for fibre and timber, both of which New Zealand had in plenty. All the varieties of flax, which the Maori had selected, cherished and tended over the centuries, and all their expertise in cultivating the plants, extracting the fibre and making the strongest of natural ropes or the softest of feather cloaks, was there for the taking. Timber, too, of every sort: kauri, totara, rimu, matai, kahikatea, the hard softwood relics of the forest, which had once covered Gondwana. Down they came; the wood that wasn't exported was put to local use and more, much more was burned where it fell.

It had taken the Maori fires 800 years to reduce the forest cover of Aotearoa from seventy-five to fifty-five per cent of all the land, but it required only eighty years of European sovereignty to slash and burn as much again. Early writings of the period observe, often with great sadness, how for days and even weeks on end, the autumn sky would be darkened with smoke, and the night sky lit with the red glow of burning forest.

The Treaty House, Waitangi.

The Meeting House, Waitangi.

161

Much of the already-degraded kauriland and the newly worked forest was reworked for subfossil wood and kauri gum, the former to augment the dwindling supplies, the latter to make all manner of things, including linoleum. I can well remember lino, cold and unyielding on the bedroom floor of my youth, and the joy when we were able to afford a wool carpet.

There was also real gold in the hills and alluvial plains, from the gumlands of the Coromandel down through Nelson, Marlborough and the West Coast to Central Otago, and out it came. Gold export began in 1857, and since then the panning, drifting, dredging and high-pressure hosing has wrested thirty million ounces from the ground, leaving more than 60,000 hectares desolate, if not derelict.

It was the new concentrations of humanity (although some historians have added the prefix sub-) around the shore stations, ports, lumbercamps and mines which hastened the opening-up of land for other, more value-added purposes. Sealers, whalers, sawyers, flaxmillers and miners all need shelter, food and clothing. Small-holdings carved out of the local bush at first met local needs, but if you can find an overseas market for wood and gold, why not for wool and the gold of butter and fatstock?

The Maori had not long gone from their forest homes when sheep and cows began to take their place, in open fields with grass planted between the stumps of forest trees. To date, an estimated eight billion animal-years' worth of grazing, treading and trampling, urinating and manuring.

The tussocklands were obvious and early victims, and the wealth of the great runholders who pushed their sheep up into the mountains, and who built Christ-church and Dunedin, also laid the foundations of catastrophe. Repeated annual fires, mistakenly lit in good faith to induce new growth, sapped the regenerative strength of even the toughest native grasses. John Buchanan of the New Zealand Geological Survey wrote in 1868: 'Nothing can show greater ignorance of grass conservation than the repeated burning of the pasture in arid districts, which is so frequently practised . . . it is no wonder that many of the runs require eight acres to feed a single sheep. The natives retreated and erosion set in on an unprecedented scale.'

Muskets were doing for the New Zealand Land Wars what the three-wheeled, double-furrow lever plough and draughthorses did for the escalating onslaught on the environment. The wheat boom of the 1870s turned much of the dry east of the South Island from tussock to cereals, and the end of the Land Wars led to the opening up of the Waikato and Waipa lowlands, which became the richest dairylands in the world.

The development of the land around Taranaki, though typical of many, at least includes one native plant in its story. The jew's-ear fungus grows in abundance on trees like karaka, mahoe and kawakawa in wet forests. A Chinese goldminer turned pedlar and grocer saw potential in exporting the fungus back to his homeland, where it was in great demand in soups for flavouring. He paid the local farmers threepence a pound for collecting it from the woods, which they were then struggling to tame and turn into smallholdings and farmsteads. By the mid-1880s Chew Chong's exports were grossing £70,000 a year. Recycling this already-recycled woodland wealth, he further helped the still-struggling local farmers. Having got a toehold on the land,

Jew's ear fungus.

these cow cockies, as they came to be known, could feed their families from among the sea of burned stumps. They needed money for development, and the only way to get it was to sell surplus milk, but most of the markets were far away and transport was in a very primitive state. Chew Chong took the surplus off their hands, building factories and a creamery called Jubilee in honour of Queen Victoria. By 1855 the first dairy co-operative in Taranaki had opened and was called what else but Moa. In 1889 Chew Chong, now one of the most respected members of the local community, added the boon of refrigeration to his dairy plant and won a silver cup for his export butter at the Dunedin Exhibition. From this point, it was all systems grow, as refrigerated steamships moved butter, cheese, lamb and mutton across a hungry world. Chew Chong went into the butter- and cheese-box industry and down came those resin-free, odourless, soft kahikatea trees, which stood in the way of development of more flat land for agriculture.

There were, of course, problems all along the line. Even the best land lacked nitrate, phosphate and lime, and the land that brought bankruptcy to some, enriched others. Out of the riches came new middleman professions, and solutions to the problems were researched in the new colleges and universities up and down the land. Pastures were better drained, sown with exotic grasses like perennial rye, while white clover added at least the three-leaf magic of root nodules and symbiotic nitrogen fixation. Greenswards got greener and pioneering eyes turned towards the hills, the battlefield of the next century. Those forest-covered hills of the north proved the most intractable.

The First World War got in the way, as 100,000 men went to fight for the King in countries far away. Those lucky enough to return from one war joined the battle at home, the battle to put sheep on the hills. Cut the bush all summer with axe and saw, and then, if there was a dry autumn day with just sufficient wind blowing in the right direction, set the dried-out bush on fire. It was back-breaking, lonely work. Just how many kiwis were consumed in these conflagrations is anyone's guess, but there was little time for concern, or even for rest. The grass-clover seed mix had to be spread by hand while the ash was still warm. Then a quick prayer for rain — 'but please, God, not too much', for that could wash away the seed, ash, soil and all. If all went well and spring sprung green between the blackened stumps, a long trek down to the nearest bank was the order of the next few days. Withdrawal of meagre capital, or credit if deemed possible, a brief visit to friends and perhaps a potential wife, then back with a mob of dry ewes to trample and consolidate the soil, setting a new pattern of recycling in motion.

If only the scientists had found out just a little sooner that the wasting disease that killed so many sheep was due to lack of cobalt. If only world demand and prices for agricultural produce had stayed high. If only the Great Depression hadn't been so great, then the Bridge to Nowhere would have led to somewhere other than Heart-break Hills. The Bridge to Nowhere, and all those other bridges that have long since rolled into a tangle of rusting wires, led both to and from small, vibrant farm communities. Supplied via the Wanganui River, which was crowded with boats as far as Taumaranui, the settlers walked in with supplies to their new farms, full of life and hope.

We did it the easy way and flew low over the hills, now clad in regrowth forest, and filmed small groups of feral pigs, sheep and even cattle, which shied away from the helicopter's noise. Landing in what must have been the home field of the largest farm of the Mangaparua catchment, I was left with the silence of the past as the chopper roared off to refuel. The drains had long since blocked and the exotic grasses were being replaced by sedge and tussock. The garden had run amok, and only the toughest plants had survived in the shade of a now-immense hedge of macrocarpa.

Of the house and household, a chimney stack, a rusted cooking pot and the base of an Alfa-Laval hand-cranked milk separator were all that remained. There was no noise of children, cattle nor cottage industry, only the wind through the macrocarpa and the background buzz of bees, perhaps still searching for those nectar-filled flowers that had once graced a herbaceous border.

The return of the helicopter awoke me to the knowledge that it took the surplus of another war to conquer the hill slopes of Moa's Ark. The matériel of the Second World War provided explosives to rip roots from stump-infested paddocks, great machines to bulldoze and shape the land as draughthorses never could, while above, around and over flew aircraft to add the final touch — phosphate fertilisers. The bird riches of three tiny islands, Nauru, Ocean and Christmas, themselves depopulated and torn by other people's wars, were up for grabs: rich deposits of phosphate, laid down by the excretions of billions of seabirds which had, over the years, used the coral islands for resting. Surplus nutrients from the great cycle of Pacific life were there, latent, ready to be put to use on another group of Pacific islands.

The Bridge to Nowhere.

There was no more digging and spreading by hand. It was the top-dressing victory roll that put green grass where the native bush had clung on in defiance of all ground attack. In time, the old war-surplus planes were replaced by purpose-built airframes, and even helicopters, complete with spray booms, with ground crews that could put the strike force back in the air in minutes, if not seconds.

In a world weary of war, with rebuilding nations demanding food, a new affluence of agriculture kept the top-dressers in the field, drawing on the reserves of phosphate as if there was no tomorrow. Cobalt, copper, molybdenum and zinc, all the micronutrients identified by agroscience, were added to the mix to smooth green-sward across the hills. Catastrophes of the past, like those caused by the heavy rains of 1938, were a whole world war away, and the next thirty-year flood was at least twenty years into an affluent future. The independence of Nauru and the problems posed by the European Common Market were but shadows on the horizons of Commonwealth.

With farms in full production, the top-dressing circus perfected a new and more sinister act. To their breath-taking repertoire of chemical welfare, the raining of goodies to coax and boost productivity, was added chemical warfare. Herbicides, insecticides, pesticides, rodenticides, lagomorphicides — a whole new armamentarium of agrochemicals began to target a rash of new enemies, both native and exotic, a rain of death from the skies. Moa's Ark would never again be the same, and so it was that when Cyclone Bola wreaked havoc across the North Island and dumped massive amounts of rain on Poverty Bay, causing erosion even more massive than the rains fifty years before, we could at least look at the status quo of New Zealand's vegetation as set out in a book published in 1988.

The Roll of Honour of the People's Conquest of the Vegetation Cover of New Zealand

Of the twenty-seven million hectares of available land, give or take a few, dependent upon the state of play of erosion and sea-level fluctuations:

About nine million hectares have been tamed beyond recognition and put down to pasture crops, orchards and exotic plantation.

Some five million hectares have been altered by soil improvement, drainage and planting of exotics vegetation.

Nearly thirteen million hectares are still in their natural pristine state.

If only that were true.

The sad truth is that today there is not one square metre of Moa's Ark that has not been changed by the raiders.

Raiders of the Last Ark

The list of plants and animals introduced either by accident or design onto the world's last Ark is legion and, despite the strict quarantine regulations, is increasing every year.

Some, like taro, kumara, potato, wheat, perennial rye grass, Monterey pine, pigs, sheep, goats, cows, horses, trout, dogs and Polynesian rats, were imports of necessity, for they made new lifestyles possible. Others, like deer, rabbits, possum, chamois, gorse, macrocarpa, willow and poplar, were introduced for game and landscape management. Others were brought to make the new migrants feel more at home, and here the list is long. Sparrows, thrushes, blackbirds, starlings, heather and roses, will whet your memories, while many, like mumps, chicken-pox, smallpox and Aids, rats and mice, thistles, nettles and couchgrass, just hitched a ride.

The categories are not clear-cut; people's reasons for including plants and animals in their luggage are as diverse as the people themselves. The most diverse reasons, and introductions, were probably thanks to the members of the acclimatisation societies, whose sole aim seemed to be to introduce and naturalise everything, including the kitchen sink.

There is no better window onto this world of devastation than the view from Mount Kaukau, above Wellington, on which is Television New Zealand's broadcasting mast. Below the peak, which beams news and views to the nation, is one of the finest stands of divaricating shrubs found anywhere in the country. Not just one, but a number of species and genera of several different families of flowering plants which all have a multiplicity of tiny branches. These form a protective mat within which the leaves, flowers and fruits are borne safe from the wind and from browsing animals.

Before people arrived on the scene, bringing all the other invaders with them, the only large browsers on Moa's Ark were the moas themselves. Although the moas are gone, the moa-resistant shrubs are there, fitting together like some gigantic sculpture made of steel wool and shaped by the wind to the contour of the hill: an oasis of native bush set in a wilderness of alien plants, dominated by gorse and browsed by rabbits, right down to the outskirts of the Capital. We searched and found *Peripatus* still hanging on in the decaying stump of one of the divaricating shrubs, but not for much longer; the oasis is drying up as gorse and Yorkshire fog move in. Not far away, in fact just over the range of hills, as the kokako used to fly, are a few kilometres of what remains of the Orongorongo Forest, in which scientists from the Department of Scientific and Industrial Research have, for the past twenty years, studied the effects of browsing by a large population of possums. These are islands of native vegetation in an immense sea of introduced plants.

Divaricating shrubs on Mount Kaukau,
Wellington.

The divaricating habit — *Hymenanthera alpina*.

From juvenile to adult foliage in kaikomako,
Pennantia corymbosa.

There are today very few places in New Zealand where the scourge of the possum and gorse has not reached, and it is safe to say that no part of Moa's Ark has escaped the effect of at least one or more of the raiders.

The list is too long to consider in full, so in order to appraise the truly shocking state of affairs we will simply consider an Alphabet of Concern.

Ammophila arenaria — marram grass

A stout perennial grass which loves the challenge of salt-laden sea breezes. It binds and stabilises shifting sand, thanks to long, creeping stems which root at the nodes. Master of one of the most stressful environments on earth, its beautiful blue-green leaves are rolled, shutting in the stomata and controlling water loss.

Introduced from Europe to bind the many dunes damaged by grazing, deforestation, sand mining and recreation, it has done a magnificent job, but it has ousted the native sand-binders from much of 52,000 hectares of coastline. One of the casualties has been the native pingao, a sedge used by Maori craftspeople in their finest weaving.

Blackberry — *Rubus fruticosus*

A member of the rose family, with arching stems which are armoured and rooting at the tips, and can walk across a paddock or up a stream bed. Flowers and fruit are only borne in the second year of stem growth, their tiny, almost gritty, seeds carried far and wide by birds.

A plant that would make anyone from England, Scotland, Wales or Ireland feel at home, complete with memories of scratched legs and blackberry and apple pie. Introduced for its fruit, it pockmarks New Zealand with its prickly presence and is, in places, getting out of hand.

Clematis vitalba — old man's beard

A member of the buttercup family, it behaves as a woody vine. Climbing by means of tendrils and leaf stalks, it zooms up into the highest canopy. In time the dangling liana-like stems become woody and can grow to fifty centimetres in diameter, or more. A prolific flowerer, whose fruits are topped by a silky plume which acts both as a parachute and a sail.

Introduced as an ornamental, this plant now has a real stranglehold on the native bush, especially in calcareous areas. A definite menace, old man's beard must go.

Deer — fallow, *Cervus dama dama*; red, *Cervus elaphus*; sambar, *Cervus unicolor*; wapiti, *Cervus elaphus nelsoni*

Even-toed, ungulate mammals, members of the family Cervidae, most of the males grow antlers anew each year, ready for the rutting season. From 1861 onwards there were attempts to introduce a number of species for sport and food; many were, unfortunately, a huge success. They are all browsers and now range from the tops of the mountains down to the coast, with catastrophic effects on the structure of the forest. All the most palatable understorey plants and seedlings are eaten out, regeneration is held back and, on steep slopes, erosion sets in.

Although the signs of catastrophe were demonstrated as early as 1892, the

Old man's beard climbing kahikatea trees near Taihape.

power of the hunting lobby made sure that new bloodstock and new species were imported up to 1910, and some remained protected as game animals as late as 1930. The red deer population peaked in New Zealand in 1930–45 and then declined as the forests were overgrazed.

Then, with the damage especially to the new plantations of exotic trees obvious even to the most blinkered members of the acclimatisation societies, culling on a massive scale became the order of the years ahead. An annual bag of 25,000 head was not out of the ordinary, but hardly made a dent in the overall problem. Post-Second World War days saw planes, then helicopter gunships, join in the battle. Prices for export venison — lean, healthful meat — soared, as did the demand for antler velvet for the Eastern, organic, aphrodisiac market. The forest began to heave a sigh of relief.

With such economic potential, restrictions were lifted and in 1970 the farming of deer was allowed; what had been classed as noxious pests were now classed farm stock. Many helicopter companies rose to the new challenge. Their guns filled with tranquiliser darts and their winches fitted with slings and nets, they made fortunes with outrageous acts of aerobatics, and the forests and upland pastures began to recover. But now most of the farms are up and breeding, the market is becoming satiated and there is less need to comb the hills for breeding stock. What price the forests now?

Elodea canadensis — Canadian pondweed

A member of the family of flowering plants called Hydrocharitaceae, a free-floating water plant, small pieces of which can grow with amazing rapidity. Along with its companion, *Lagarosiphon*, another oxygenator, it has been carted around the world from its home in North America to stock fish tanks and ornamental ponds. Introduced into Britain just two years after the signing of the Treaty of Waitangi, it took over the resources of rivers, lakes and canals, brought water traffic to a stand-still and even threatened the stockmarket and the Boat Race.

170

It reached New Zealand, evidently by accident, with a batch of fish eggs from Tasmania in 1865 and soon made itself at home. Although New Zealand had a unique aquatic flora, it was poor in species that thrive in well-lit flowing environments, for in their natural state most of the rivers, streams and lakes were overshadowed by forest. So, *Elodea* and *Lagarosiphon* are still doing their best to take over all water bodies, especially those enriched by farming and sewage.

Felis catus — domestic cat

A nice furry mammal, a member of the cat family, a great hunter and voracious carnivore. Just when and where the cat was first domesticated is still a matter of debate, but once the habit had caught on, everyone, including many New Zealanders, seemed to want a moggy. The native birds just did not stand a chance. It has to be admitted that the cats do help keep down the rats and mice, which also do great damage to all bird populations except the most aggressive, like weka, pukeko and kiwi.

Goats — *Capra hircus*

Another member of the even-toed, ungulate group of mammals. Difficult to tell from sheep except for the fact that their forehead is convex not concave, and that they will eat anything and everything. I quote from the *Encyclopaedia of Mammals*: 'Released on oceanic islands, goats have reduced earthly paradises to barren soil with only poor vegetation. They have and are contributing to the process of desertification.'

When goats were introduced by the early navigators, Moa's Ark was still an earthly paradise. What hope remains for the backblock bush now that goat farming is less viable and the herds are being released back into the scrub?

Another bearded invader — feral billy goat.
ROD MORRIS

Russell lupins invade a riverbed.

Heather — *Calluna vulgaris*

A diffuse, evergreen shrub that can grow up to a metre tall and probably holds the world's record for pollen production, with a prodigious sixteen million pollen grains per square metre of well-managed moorland. Beloved of grouse, bees and tartanophiles, heather was introduced for all those reasons and has taken a mighty foothold in some mighty inappropriate places, like the middle slopes of Tongariro, New Zealand's first national park. The grouse died out but the heather is blooming!

Iberis amara — candytuft

A member of the cabbage family, which gives us so many of our useful vegetables, like radish, turnip and Chinese mustard; some beautiful garden flowers, like honesty and night-scented stocks; and some real pains in the herbaceous border, like shepherd's purse and charlock.

Candytuft is usually not an aggressive weed, but it has found a niche on gold spoil in Otago, where it is doing its own bit of instant reclamation and reminding us of Ralph Waldo Emerson's claim that 'a weed is a plant whose virtues have not yet been discovered'. Likewise, a garden plant has many virtues until it escapes from captivity.

Juncus species — rushes

These members of the flowering plant family Juncaceae are perfectly adapted to grow in wet, marshy places. As across much of the world, most of New Zealand's wonderful wetlands have been drained, but it is in these betwixt-and-between dry wetlands that the rushes have rushed in and taken over from the natives. This is a habitat of great importance, where, if the wrong thing gets in, much can be crowded out and lost, blocking up the drains and increasing the cost of management.

King devil hawkweed — *Hieracium praealtum*

A member of one of the most successful groups of a very successful family of flowering plants, the Compositae, which includes the daisies and dandelions.

Hawkweeds are apomicts, which means that they can set seeds without the fuss and bother of pollination and sexual union. Set seed they do, and, once established, they just spread and spread. A real devil in the King Country and beyond, they fill up open space which used to be the domain of many rare and now endangered native plants.

Lupinus polyphyllus — Russell lupin

A native of North America, this member of the pea flower family — or rather members, because there are a number of them — came to Moa's Ark as a garden plant complete with nitrogen-fixing root nodules and pods packed with seeds. 'A nice thing to cover that odd waste corner,' it said on the packet. Unfortunately the packet was right and *Lupinus* lived up to its second name, rapidly filling all the holes and binding the shingle and gravel banks of New Zealand's famous braided rivers. Poor old black stilt and the many native plants that used to like the wide-open braided places.

Moa's Ark

Mustela erminea — stoat; *M. nivalas* — weasel; *M. furo* — ferret

Stoats are stoatally different and weasels are weasily distinguishable. Ferrets are bigger than both. All are, unfortunately, expert hunters and voracious carnivores.

Imported in 1884 to tackle the rabbit problem, stoats and weasels would have got a little cheesed off by the success of the rabbit boards (see below) if there had not also been rats, mice and, of course, native birds, on which to cut their teeth. The deadlier ferret, although a friend of gamekeepers, is a foe of even the yellow-eyed penguin, and was introduced slightly earlier than the other mustelids, in 1879.

Nodding thistle — *Carduus nutans*

Annual and perennial herbs with spirally arranged prickly leaves and dense, distinctive flowerheads bearing a wealth of wind-blown seed. Members of the daisy family.

The Order of the Thistle is borne by the honoured few, but the presence of thistles is a burden borne by many landowners, large and small. Surely they must have been brought to New Zealand by accident, not by some homesick Scot. The truth, however, is that back on crofts in Scotland, thistle leaves were used to feed farmstock, and thistledown to stuff pillows and cushions, so they could have been imported on purpose. Their only saving grace is that they sustain goldfinches, which eat their seeds and look very pretty.

Oryctolagus cuniculus — rabbit

A member of the group of mammals called Lagomorpha. Their reproductive powers are proverbial: a female can produce up to six litters a year, and young rabbits can start to breed in the year of their birth.

Introduced probably as food for sealers and gold miners, these fecund nibblers soon staked a claim on sheep runs and tussocklands. By the 1870s it was all-out war; the only ground cover left in large areas were dung pellets, and the air stank with their urine. In 1873, 33,000 pelts were exported, escalating to nine million only nine years later, when frozen carcases joined the expanding export trade. The Rabbit Nuisance Act of 1876 made it all official, and the bounty-hunting rabbiters, who were soon making more money than the farmers, jealously preserved their breeding stock.

Stoats, weasels and cats were added to the fray, and so-called rabbit fences were erected at great cost. Yet in 1924, exports stood at twenty-two million pelts and damage was so severe that something had to be done. It was not until 1947 and the setting up of the rabbit boards throughout the country, that the problem began to be contained. Ten years later, all trade in pelts and carcases was banned and bait impregnated with novel poisons began to rain down from the air. No one framed this Roger Rabbit, he came, he saw, and he took over more than half of Moa's Ark. He could do it again and, with the demise of the rabbit boards, looks likely to do so.

Possum — *Trichosurus vulpecula*

A member of the great group of pouched mammals which have their own special ark of continental dimensions, called Australia. Introduced as fur animals in the middle of the last century and protected until 1946, they are today the number one enemy of New Zealand's native forests. Expert climbers and gourmet-leaf eaters, possums survey the great green forest smorgasbord from on high and take their pick.

A Norway rat on the forest floor.
KEN MILLER

Possum, in a tree hole.
ROD MORRIS

A 'stoatally different' mustelid.
ROD MORRIS

Moa's Ark

Favourites like northern rata go first for breakfast, dinner, tea and supper until, one by one, the tastiest trees are destroyed: only then do the possums move on. The menu goes something like this: northern rata, native mistletoe, native fuschia, kamahi, kohekohe, five-finger, and so on down a list of seventy species, ending up, when forced by hunger, with even things like miro, whose leaves are full of turpentine. As the structure of the forest changes, so does the environment for all native shrubs, herbs, mosses, liverworts, lichens and, of course, birds and insects.

The possums must go, every last one of them, and the sooner the better.

Quaking grass — *Briza maxima*

A very successful member of the grass flower family. Introduced among or as a pasture grass, its silvery flower heads, which quake in the slightest breeze, now make many a European feel at home, in both the North and South Islands. It may be beautiful, but Moa's Ark would be better off without it.

Rattus rattus — black rat; *R. norvegicus* — Norway rat; *R. exulans* — kiore

Along with the mice, these are members of that most successful animal group, the rodents, which, on a world scale, number more than 500, half of all the mammalian species.

There is no doubt that the Maori introduced the kiore, or Polynesian rat, as a source of food. Thank goodness it is mainly a seed-eater, and so has had less effect on the native fauna. The rest introduced themselves, hitching lifts on ships.

Rats and mice — catastrophe: they are ecological anarchists — tough, intelligent, adaptable and prolific. Sadly, no part of New Zealand can be said to be beyond risk. One example will suffice — rats arrived by boat on Big South Cape Island, off the south coast of Stewart Island, in or before 1962, and by 1964 there were no saddlebacks, wrens, fernbirds, robins or snipe, and few bellbirds, parakeets or short-tailed bats left. Many of the special insects had gone and the plants had been badly damaged.

Sweet briar — *Rosa rubiginosa*

Shrubs, one to four metres high, armed with strong prickles and producing many flowers, which can pollinate themselves and produce a myriad of seed.

Wherever the English went, they just had to take their roses along. There was, however, no real need to take the wild ones, despite the fact that their hips produce syrup rich in vitamin C and they make you feel at home in the hedgerow. For better or for worse, they got there and the Wars of the Roses are waging battle royal across huge stretches of farmland, particularly in the South Island.

Thymus vulgaris — wild thyme

Low, aromatic shrubs, almost fifty different species, and all were confined to the north temperate Old World. Originally from the Mediterranean, it is the plant which gives Central Otago not only its colour, but its aroma too.

It is such a prolific producer of seeds that, when the wind shakes the seed pods, the whole crop hisses — a rattle of death for many native plants. Beloved of the introduced honey-bees, it gives the spring honey such a strong taste that the combs are left to feed the hive. Another take-over export.

Sweet briar and wild thyme rampant in Central Otago.

Ulex europaeus — gorse

A member of the pea flower family, with leaves modified into very nasty spines. It was first introduced as a hedging plant to keep farmstock in place. Its spines and its lifestyle soon began to keep the stock out as it exploded across paddocks and newly cleared bushland. Nitrogen-fixing bacteria in its root nodules, and explosive fruits, which shower seeds far and wide, gave it a tremendous advantage over native and exotic plants alike. It now holds its dark-green and golden-yellow sway over no less than 260,000 hectares, one per cent of Moa's Ark. It might prove a good nurse plant for native bush plants, but the evidence is not yet clear.

Vespula germanica — German wasp

The distinguishing marks of the German wasp are three black dots on its face and the yellow band on the front of its abdomen. Introduced by accident and established only in 1945, these nectar-drinkers are in direct competition with the native nectar-feeding birds and insects. The best way to see them is to look at the stream of honeydew which pours from the trunks of the southern beech. The invaders are everywhere, spreading throughout the web of life and reducing the chances of survival of many animals. They are also a perishing nuisance at picnics.

Wandering jew — *Tradescantia virginiana*

A member of the tropical flower family Commelinaceae, and a favourite household plant with the unfortunate habit of reproducing by fragmentation, which means that if a bit is broken off it will take root and grow again. Great for giving a piece to your next-door neighbour, but almost impossible to get rid of once it has a hold.

It was first introduced into Britain from Virginia by the Tradescants, the fathers of English gardening. Thank goodness English winters are too cold for it, so it stays indoors — not so in New Zealand, where it was introduced into the Manawatu and now smothers regenerating seedlings in forest remnants throughout the North Island.

Cord grass invading Whangarei Harbour.

Wild ginger in Northland.

Spartina **x** *townsendii* — hybrid cord grass

A stout perennial grass which excels as a mud-binder between the tides. The 'x' in its Latin name means that it is a hybrid; it arose by the chance meeting of two other cord grasses in Southampton Water in 1862. Like many other hybrids, it is large and aggressive, and took over Southampton Water and is still engulfing Britain. Since that time it has been carted round the world to stabilise estuarine muds, with catastrophic results for the local flora and fauna, and especially for the wading birds that probe soft muds for their food.

Estuaries are the kidneys of the land and the ovaries of the seas, cleansing the water that flows down the rivers, and allowing many fish and shellfish to complete parts of their life cycle within their rich and sheltered waters. Many estuaries are now menaced by this invader, and in those areas where short-sighted people are still reclaiming New Zealand's unique subtropical mangroves, *Spartina* will spread with far-reaching results.

Yorkshire fog — *Holcus lanatus*

A soft, densely hairy perennial grass, which, when growing en masse and caught by the early morning or evening sun, looks like mist rising from the ground. Introduced as a pasture grass, it has brought a frog to the throat of many a homesick emigrant from Yorkshire or the northern dales of England, and has squeezed out many a native plant in New Zealand.

Zingiberaceae — the ginger family

Hedychium gardnerianum, the false ginger, is the nearest I can get to a Z. It is a really nasty invader of stream edges and swampland in native bush of the warm North Island. Introduced for its tolerance of waterlogging and the beauty of its flowers, it is now a source of great concern throughout the Auckland region and in Northland.

A, right down to Z (and I only really cheated with the last one), these are just a few of more than 2,000 Raiders of the Last Ark which have wrought, and will continue to wreak, havoc on the native plants and animals, causing irreparable damage and enormous expenditure until they are finally brought under control.

Of the animals in the Alphabet of Concern, probably possums and wasps are the worst because they alter their environment in both gross and subtle ways. Of the plants, *Clematis vitalba*, *Tradescantia* and ginger are sufficiently aggressive to smother whole plant communities — they must go too.

Many of the invaders will never be controlled and are likely to change irrevocably the biota of New Zealand. A new balance will be struck, and the retreat of the original vegetation will continue. There is never going to be enough money to manage the whole country in an ecologically sensitive way — perhaps the best we can hope for is to control the worst of the damaging species and let history and succession take their course.

Kaingaroa Forest

Despite the fact that around half of Moa's Ark has been refitted for the benefit of one class of passenger, *Homo sapiens*, and the other half has to a greater or lesser extent been badly mauled by the raiders which spilled over from the first-class decks, New Zealand still has many wonders of the natural world: Rotorua, Milford Sound, Taranaki, Stephens Island, Waipoua, Whirinaki, Mount Cook, to mention just seven of the first twenty-six windows into its natural history.

It is sadly true to say that many of these have survived only because of their remoteness and the fact that they had little to offer in the way of economic return for farming or forestry. It is also true to say that, thanks to neglect and the combined attack of the raiding hordes, enormous amounts of money are now having to be spent to hold not only them but the rest of Moa's Ark together as a viable unit fit for the survival of its people and wildlife alike.

It is no good blaming the early acclimatisationists, or any of the other pioneers. They could not live off native bush alone, and so they came to regard it as a green, monotonous wasteland, an enemy which had to be destroyed if they were to gain survival. Whether we like the end result or not, we must all agree that it was their sheer hard work and determination which performed the miracle that allowed New Zealand's human population to top the three million mark and helped to feed and clothe two post-war worlds.

To make way for farmlands, at least ten million hectares of native forest and bush were destroyed. About half of the kauri, rimu, totara, kahikatea and the other native timbers were burned, and half of the rest was put to good use in the fencing of farms, the construction of dams and railways, the building of woolsheds and homes and the boxing of butter, apples and cheese for export. Timber was, and is, big business, so in 1919 this advertisement appeared in all leading newspapers:

'A chief inspector of forestry is required by the New Zealand Government. Salary £600 per annum increasing to £700. Candidates should be graduates from a school of forestry of recognised standing. Full particulars and forms of application obtainable from the High Commissioner for New Zealand, 45 The Strand, London, by whom completed applications will be received up to the 20th January 1920.'

Only six years later, the Chief Inspector of Forests (a Canadian called Leon MacIntosh Ellis), warned the Government that at the current rate of exploitation, only forty years' supply of marketable timber was left in New Zealand. Horrified at the prospects, the nation, under the zeal and direction of Ellis, set about the awesome task of providing wood for the future by planning to plant no less than 121,500 hectares (they called them 300,000 acres in those days) of plantation within ten years. An impossible task! And it would have been, but for one species of tree, an

A plantation of *Pinus radiata*.

introduction from the Monterey Peninsula of California; its name, *Pinus radiata*.

Why, I ask, with all the fantastic native timber trees to hand, did the foresters opt for an exotic, and why the Monterey pine? It may be just that exotic trees, or at least the vast majority of them, grow extraordinarily well when planted in New Zealand: no one can dispute the fact.

When the homesick acclimatisationists brought in their oaks from England, poplars from Lombardy, gums from Australia and macrocarpa and pines from Monterey, they all stood back in amazement as jealous neighbours looked over the hedge and said, 'Don't they grow well?' A sentiment re-echoed much later by Richard St Barbe Baker, the founder of Men of the Trees. Little wonder, then, that despite the dinosaurian size of many of the native trees, the settlers looked with scorn at their seedlings and saplings, which grew only very slowly beneath their parents' shade and on their accumulated litter.

Consequently, in went the macrocarpa, which could be trimmed into an impenetrable hedge, and up went the Monterey pine to throw almost instant shade across sun-drenched paddocks: you could almost hear them grow. When it came to plantations, there was little need to look any further than the dominants of the wind-breaks and shady copses, the cones of which were already bursting with a good crop of seed: seed which, in many places, could be planted out directly in straight rows across the promised land — no need for nursery or fertiliser, just bung 'em in and up they go.

All the wildest expectations were exceeded as the new plantations began to produce five to ten times more timber per hectare than the main production forests of Scandinavia and Canada. *Pinus radiata* was here to stay, and in a very big way.

Leon MacIntosh Ellis would have been appalled at the idea of such myopic reliance on a single species, for the dangers of fire, disease and market forces were enormous. Plantation technology at least quelled the fears of the first and perhaps the last, but two raiders did their best to destroy Ellis's dream of future self-sufficiency in timber.

A wood wasp, complete with self-made arboricide, arrived from America in the 1920s, in (would you believe it?) imported wood. The arboricide killed the wood and was injected, along with the wasps' eggs and the spores of wood-rotting fungi which softened it up, ready for the larvae of the wood wasp itself. By the late 1940s, the larvae were busily chewing up the annual wood production across 100,000 hectares of prime plantation. Fortunately, better plantation husbandry and, more recently, biological warfare has got the wasp under control.

In 1964, needle blight fungus began to devastate plantations across both the North and South Islands. Air attack using copper-based fungicides was the only way to save the day over 40,000 hectares of growing timber. The cost was high but, with the industry and all those jobs at stake, it was well worth the investment. Outbreaks of the fungus continue from time to time, but are contained by aerial spraying — technology again.

The timber industry, too, has had its ups and downs. In the early days, pine was considered too resinous to compete with spruce and larch for pulping, and the wood was too knotty for structural and other purposes. With the giant Kaingaroa Forest coming on stream at an incredible thirty years of age, the menace of wood borers in, and of hurricanes on, the tall trees, already past their prime, increased. As did competition from cheaper Third World resources. Something had to be done. Under new government initiatives, industry took up the challenge and the sweet promises of downstream jobs and export revenue began to be fulfilled. New towns and enterprises grew up within the expanding forest lands, and the pulp, paper and newsprint mills began to turn the potential of the plantations into export assets. The knotty problem of unbrashed trees was at last solved by the expenditure of more money in management. Gangs worked throughout the best plantations, brashing — cleaning the trunks of the lateral branches which caused the knots to develop. So the production of clearwood, free of knots and other growth defects which would weaken the timber, made it a much more marketable proposition. Likewise pressure, or rather vacuum, impregnation of the timber with fungicides and insecticides has helped clinch pine's acceptability for structural purposes.

Pinus radiata is a story of great success, for today, of the 121,000 hectares of exotic forest, no less than 96,000 hectares are dominated by this one species. A living, growing resource of immense value, which has saved much more native forest than it has replaced — for there is little doubt that without Leon MacIntosh Ellis's foresight and forthright approach, much more of the native forests of Moa's Ark would have been destroyed, and New Zealand's balance of payments would be even further in the red. Also, who can hazard a guess at all the other raiders that might have arrived in Moa's Ark with the timber that would have had to be imported in order to make up the deficit?

What are the statistics of this fantastic resource in terms of just one upmarket, high-value-added product? The Lockwood building technique (dare I say magic?) produces thermally efficient houses. These are not only earthquake-proof but, being of great beauty, charm and diversity, can stand up to market forces anywhere. As an example, we will take a middle-of-the-range, 100-square-metre, thermally efficient Lockwood home. We will call it the Lockwood 100, and the sums look like this:

One Lockwood 100 requires 31.35 cubic metres of timber.

One average hectare of plantation grows 20 cubic metres of timber per year, but unfortunately, only half can be used in a Lockwood house.

Therefore, one average hectare of plantation produces 0.32 Lockwood 100s per year.

Therefore, 1,150 hectares of plantation grows one Lockwood 100 each day.

Therefore, every day, Kaingaroa Forest grows 695.65 Lockwood 100s, representing a new home for every New Zealander once every twelve years.

A Lockwood house on the move.

What an amazing renewable resource these pines are! If only the plantations provided a good habitat for native plants and animals, there could be few grumbles. But they do not, and the thought of *Pinus radiata* or any other exotic marching across another 100,000 hectares of the countryside raises the hackles of many people.

The question must therefore be asked, why not plant some of the native trees as commercial crops? It would certainly be fantastic to be growing 695.65 kauri houses every day, and there is a lot of now-degraded land on which kauri used to, and still could, grow. The answers come back thick and fast, the first one being: 'We do not have the plantation technology for kauri.' Well, neither did Ellis have the plantation technology worked out for pine when he laid down his plans, and if he did, why did he overlook its resinous and knotty nature? The truth is that the technology was worked out en route, and we could do the same for kauri.

The second negative always quoted is that kauri grows too slowly. Actual comparisons make for interesting reading — one hectare of pine plantation containing 300 trees grows 20 cubic metres per year, so each tree must grow 0.066 cubic metres of wood per year. To compare that with a kauri tree we have to look at living trees in a kauri forest, and the obvious example is the biggest and oldest living kauri. Tane Mahuta still stands in Waipoua forest and the guide reminds you that it is around 1,200 years old and its trunk volume is 244.5 cubic metres. A little bit of mathematics tells you that, providing these statistics are correct, Tane Mahuta has put on an average of 0.21 cubic metres of wood every year throughout its long lifetime. As far as I can see, the only part of the statistics that can be wrong is the age of the tree. In order to reduce the growth rate of the Lord of the Forest to that of *Pinus radiata* pampered by plantation technology, Tane Mahuta's age must be at least 3,600 years, which would make it one of the oldest trees in the world. Add to this the fact that all trees grow faster in their youth than after reaching maturity, when their growth rate slows considerably, and it looks as if kauri grows three times faster than Monterey pine.

In conclusion, all I suggest is that it must be worth rethinking the case for commercially planting kauri and the other native trees. Now is the time to select the right genetic stock from the great trees we still have left, develop the plantation technology and reap the benefit in the future. Thank goodness some research is going on, though we must wait with fingers crossed to see 100,000 hectares of degraded land brought back into native timber production.

I can almost hear the supporters of exotic forestry saying, 'Even if we did what the greenies say, they would never let us cut the trees down when they came to harvest time.' My reply is, surely it is worth a try.

WINDOW 29

Eastwoodhill Arboretum

If you want proof that exotic trees grow well in New Zealand, even in place with the unlikely name of Poverty Bay, then make a pilgrimage to Eastwoodhill Arboretum, near Gisborne.

I had read a lot about Eastwood Hill, I had even seen pictures of it, but on 19 February 1989, I saw it for myself, and what a shock! No, not a shock of disappointment, for it lived up to all my expectations, but one of amazement at how the vision of one individual has created such an oasis of hope in such a blasted landscape.

The hills all about were in tatters, the scars of erosion glaring white in the hot summer sun. En route from the airport I was regaled with stories of the Cyclone Bola catastrophe of 1988. Of cloudbursts and landslips, when even some of the richest farmers down on the sweet flat lands of the riverside had their hopes and their livelihoods obliterated, as mud and liquid pumice poured off the hills, down towards the sea. Shelterbelts on the lowlands had done their bit protecting the orchards, vineyards and crops, and the vast majority were doing well, but up on the hills there was hardly a patch of shelter in sight and little, if any, native bush. A scene much more reminiscent of the degraded lands of a Third World country, where people are starving, than of one of the greatest agricultural nations in the world; a scene every New Zealander should be thoroughly ashamed of. I was also told that these problems had their roots in a past of deforestation and overgrazing of the catchments, which left them naked and prone to the ravages of nature. No wonder it's called Poverty Bay.

The East Coast has had its share of major environmental disasters. On 3 February 1931, in the midst of a drought-stricken summer, the east coast of the North Island was shaken by a tremendous earthquake. The shock flattened the city of Napier and many other places were damaged. Then, in 1938, the coast of Poverty Bay received one of its world-class short, sharp rainstorms. Small streams rose overnight by as much as nineteen metres, and the soil of the whole catchment of the Mangatu, and parts of the Waipaoa Rivers, flowed downhill towards the sea. In the centre of the infamous Tarndale Slip, the soils continued to flow for the next twenty years. Two months later the same happened to the Hawke's Bay coast, where torrential rain caused hillsides to spew mud and bridges to wash out to sea. In places, bare slip scars covered more than half the landscape.

All the bulldozers in New Zealand could not have caused such havoc, and all the machinery of the Public Works Department, under the command of its Director, Bob Semple, could not put the landscape back together again. Everyone laid the blame at the feet of everyone else, The Second World War became the excuse for non-action, overgrazing by deer became the scapegoat, and a programme of deer culling

Devastation caused by Cyclone Bola in the hills behind Poverty Bay.
MIKE SINGLE, TVNZ

The land stains the sea after Cyclone Bola: Waipaoa River, Poverty Bay.
MIKE HOCKEY, NZ TIMBERLANDS LTD

was put forward as the real answer. Nowadays we recognise that deer can only worsen the effect of naturally wetter and windier periods. The most recent studies suggest that up to seven periods of accelerated erosion have occurred in the last 1,800 years.

Back in 1938, one man came to the rescue. Lance McCaskill had first-hand experience of the soil conservation methods developed in the United States after the 'dust bowl' years of the earlier 1930s. Using *Pinus radiata*, he and his team of green-fingered visionaries began to knit the ravaged landscapes back together. They did not totally succeed, and to this day the Tarndale Slip still bleeds pumice whitewash to taint the river and the sea.

In the midst of all this death and destruction, one green oasis of hope had not only remained intact but had grown in size — Eastwoodhill. The arboretum owes its existence to William Cook, who was haunted by the fear that all the beauty of the great estates of Europe, laid out with trees and plants drawn from the whole of the Northern Hemisphere and beyond, would be destroyed, lost by the uncaring attitude of greedy, stupid people. So, on land he had purchased in rolling country situated in the Ngata district near Gisborne, he started to create an oasis, a Garden of Eden, held together by the best of the world's plants he had seen and heard about.

William Cook worked with his garden until he died in 1967, importing the best genetic stock he could from nurserymen and botanic gardens the world over. He and his gardeners potted, planted and planned. When drought threatened their tree nurseries, they carried water by the bucket to wean seedlings into saplings and saplings into truly magnificent trees. Indeed, the rates of growth of trees as diverse as English oak and Chinese maples, ash and liquidamber have amazed visitors. 'Hardwood trees can't grow that fast,' the sceptics said, until they came and believed their astounded eyes. It is a truly wonderful place, ranking alongside the great arboreta of the world. The best? Well, I haven't seen a better one in the Southern Hemisphere.

In his time, William Cook imported some 5,000 different species and varieties of trees to his garden. Not all thrived in the conditions around Poverty Bay, but more than 3,000 did, and the vast majority of those did very well. Many of these trees are now rare both in cultivation and in the wild. Fortunately for New Zealand, and for the world, this enterprising experiment did not die with William Cook. The whole property and the burden of looking after such an international treasurehouse was taken on by a local businessman — H. B. Williams. Working with his family, he restored much of Eastwoodhill's waning grandeur and in 1975 gave it to the state and a trust board, which has carried on the vital work.

So I stood in what can truly be called an international cathedral of trees with a crowd of some 650 Friends of Eastwoodhill. I didn't really need to say anything, for the types of trees swaying gently in the summer breeze said it all: 283 camellias, 103 oaks, 97 maples, 75 cherries and peaches, 57 pines, 50 crabapples, 43 rowans and whitebeams, 42 magnolias, 33 firs, 31 junipers, 29 birches, 26 ashes, 26 poplars, 21 spruce, 21 hollies, 16 beeches, 15 limes and a considerable number of azaleas and rhododendrons. What a collection! Go see it for yourself at any time of the year, for it changes season by season. Even if you can't make the trip, think of the vision of one man who turned an open, rapidly degrading paddock into an oasis of hope, not only for Poverty Bay but for the world.

The dream of William Douglas Cook lives on, for it is the dream of the present director and the Friends of Eastwoodhill to expand the collection to include as many of the trees of the Northern Hemisphere as possible, safe, far away from radioactive fallout, acid rain and the like. Now I have met the Friends of Eastwoodhill, I know it's going to happen: a genetic bank with which to heal not only the slopes of Poverty Bay but help with the problems of a ravaged world.

We must turn back the tide of deforestation and desertification and we can do it only if we have the genetic potential of the trees to help us on our way. Not just *Pinus radiata* and eucalypts, but wonderful hardwoods, which include those native trees that grow as fast as pines and produce shelter and timber of greater quality and value. New forests of great trees can be grown in the most ravaged and unpromising lands, for there in the distance, beyond Eastwoodhill, holding the healing hills together, is a forest of *Pinus radiata*, mostly unshaken by Cyclone Bola, just ready for the first productive cut — and thereby hangs another whole range of problems.

However carefully the logging operations are carried out, some erosion will occur, and should a bad rain coincide with the operation, the downwash could be enormous. The backlash will also be expensive, for some of New Zealand's farmers have turned the flatlands of Poverty Bay into the richest land in the country, producing grapes, kiwifruit and many other fruits. They look to the hills whence cometh their irrigation water, but they know they can do without the whitewash. The effects of the next cyclone, exacerbated by logging in the hills, may well be so devastating as to fall beyond the terms of insurance. Who should pay for the damage caused by acts of God such as Cyclone Bola?

Not far away, at the other end of the Colenso Track, which crosses the Ruahine Ranges to the Manawatu, experiments are under way which may help to solve even this problem. In a back lot of Massey University campus, itself overflowing with trees both exotic and native, several fields of one university farm have been given over to heavy cropping with trees.

There is no doubt that the world is crying out for wood and wood fibre. With the finite resources of non-renewable fossil energy and the grave doubts as to the safety and economics of nuclear fuel, many nations are carrying out experiments to determine the efficacy of growing tree crops for fuelwood and as a source of pulp, fibre and chemicals. A good example is Sweden, where 50,000 hectares of willow have been planted as part of an on-going national project. Their research programmes have shown that fuelwood has the potential not only to replace a significant proportion of their heating oil imports, but also to partly substitute for nuclear energy — and the Swedish nuclear energy programme is going to be phased out by the year 2010, following a national referendum in 1982, reinforced by the accident at Chernobyl in 1985.

All this information comes pouring out of Ralph Sims, the director of the Massey University project. He also reminds you that New Zealand has said a big no to atomic power and that he knows gas reserves could be exhausted in eighteen years. He then proudly opens the gate and lets you into his coppice woodland.

Eastwoodhill Arboretum, an island of trees in a grazed landscape.
MARION MacKAY

Coppicing is an ancient form of woodland management, which provided medieval Britain, and also the first phase of the Industrial Revolution, with the energy it needed. All the trees grown for coppicing are able to resprout when cut off at the base. The products are poles of rather precise length and thickness, depending on the tree species used, and the duration of the coppice rotation. Exactly what the chip-board manufacturers, the pulp works and the woodburning stove addicts ordered: a saleable, easily handled product from a perennial crop, which keeps its roots firmly in the ground and hence holds the soil on the catchment. What is more, the multi-stemmed, bushy trees are not as susceptible to windthrow as tall, single-stemmed, or standard, trees. Ideal for erosion control, ideal for shelterbelts, ideal for catchment management and farm income.

The trees most readily managed in Britain for coppice are oak, hazel and sweet chestnut, and with 103 different varieties of oaks at Eastwoodhill from which to select, it could be all systems grow. A good oak coppice in England, with a twenty-year cycle, might produce two tonnes of wood per hectare per year.

'Now stand back for a surprise,' said Ralph. (I couldn't actually see him at this point, because of the density of all the trees growing around and towering above me.)

'This crop is three years old.' I didn't believe him, and he went on, 'It will produce on a two-year rotation' — impossible, I thought — 'sixty tonnes per hectare per year.'

'You're pulling my leg,' I said; but no, it is all scientific fact and the tree in question is Tasmanian blue gum.

Other plots were under willows, poplars, native beech and, of course, other gums. No conifers, because the vast majority of them do not resprout once cut. The rates of growth in the other plots were not as high as the blue gum, but they were still a spectacular potential investment.

The reason for this remarkable growth-rate lies in the warm, wet, temperate climate of New Zealand, much warmer and much more temperate than Britain or even Tasmania.

New Zealanders use some 25,800 gigawatt hours of electricity each year. In order to produce that amount of blue-gum energy, a coppice plantation with an area of 500,000 hectares would be needed! Impossible, impractical, well yes, but already much of New Zealand's energy is produced by hydropower, a renewable resource which does not produce carbon dioxide, the greenhouse gas, which is mopped up and put into short-term store by coppice. The limiting factor is likely to be nutrients, for even the Tasmanian blue gum cannot grow on pure water alone, and NPK, lime and remineralisation will be necessary to keep the crop growing and the soil free from the problems of depletion and acidification.

Some answers to these problems appear to be coming from a rather strange place, the meatworks at Oringi, where 100 hectares of gum coppice is being planted in flood irrigation land adjacent to the works. Not only should the trees reduce the groundwater pollution problem, which is already evident under the present pasture regime (the grass doesn't take up all the nutrients from the slurry), but they will also provide an economic alternative for part or perhaps all of their $250,000 annual coal bill. From small but meaty beginnings, great things may grow, for the Auckland

Regional Council, no less, is evaluating the potential of coppice gums to reduce sewage-disposal problems and simultaneously to alleviate the local domestic fuel-wood scarcity. An urban working coppice woodland, complete with wildlife, right on your own doorstep.

If you can produce at least some of fuel in this way, why not short-fibre production for high-quality paper, with the residues shredded and used for energy production. Trees are versatile things, you know!

At the moment, much of this raw material comes from native beech woods, often in remote areas with problems of soil erosion and degradation, areas that should be managed and developed for much less destructive purposes. Work is going on apace and the future looks bright for productive catchment management. Hill slopes rejuvenated with coppice provide a perennial crop with minimal disturbance and erosion. With all the trees at Eastwoodhill to use as experimental gene bank, and all the genetic potential of the native trees that respond to coppice management to select from, the first commercial crops should soon keep the home fires burning.

But I am jumping the gun into the future. At the moment it is back to the drawing board of conservation, feet firmly on the decks of Moa's Ark.

PART FOUR

*Refloating
the Ark*

◀ Late afternoon sun touches Moa's Ark — looking west from the Surville Cliffs to Cape Reinga.

WINDOW 30

Conservation Kiwi-wise

Like the Z in my Alphabet of Concern, this chapter is a bit of a cheat, for it is not a window in this book's sense of the word but an eye-opener. For the locals who know it already, I apologise, but I want the rest of the world to know the facts of New Zealand's best-kept secret: of how she, at this crucial point in the earth's history, leads the world in her commitment to conservation. How did it all come about?

As long ago as 1840, a mechanism for reserving lands was laid down on Governor Hobson's instructions. The Governor was permitted to protect areas of land from alienation and use them for special purposes, the erection of government buildings and the development of docks, harbours and the like. Under the Land Act of 1877, reserves for the growth and preservation of timber were introduced, though they were for timber production rather than conservation. Even then, five years earlier an anonymous review paper entitled 'The Ornithology of New Zealand', published in the scientific journal *Nature*, decried the extent of the 'acclimatisation mania' which was ousting the native birds. The creation of the Tongariro National Park was first gazetted in 1894 after the passing of the 1892 Land Act, which allowed the creation of scenery reserves and flora and fauna reserves.

The fifty years of boom and bust development from 1840 left a legacy of destruction and despoliation, out of which grew a more subtle approach to land use. One of the pioneers of this new thinking was an extraordinary explorer called Charlie Douglas, who was the first to chart virtually every South Westland river valley and range north of Fiordland in the 1890s. Douglas, along with a few others, realised that the most profitable form of exploitation of these remote treasures lay in the preservation of the lands and landscapes. 'The mines they intend to develop in the future are the gold and silver in the pockets of the tourists. No more roads for diggers but tracks to waterfalls and glaciers.'

The world-famous Milford Track was developed and opened in the 1880s, and local goldmen, like Peter and Alex Graham, swapped their shovels for ice-picks and led the new tourists through the native bush of river valleys to glaciers and high peaks. The tourist demand was there, and in came gentlemen and lady climbers from the British Alpine Club, and the Victorian trampers and walkers, who glowed and perspired their way to a place in the well-kept record books. They came to these far-flung corners of the earth to seek inspiration from New Zealand's awesome natural beauty. Each struggling settlement on the fringe of this natural wonderland developed its own tourist guiding tradition, and large wooden hotels sprang up in idyllic alpine and bush settings. Great climbs were accomplished, and duly recorded in adventure books, which sold well back in the cities and in Europe. The books advertised the

tourism potential of New Zealand and stirred thoughts of profitable enterprise and of conservation in the minds of many. Magnificent watercolours, sketches and large plate photographs added to the flow of information and concern. So it was that 1901 saw 607,501 hectares in the vicinity of Arthur's Pass set aside as a national park reserve. In 1902, 900,000 hectares of Fiordland became the Sounds National Park. Both were then enlarged and renamed as Arthur's Pass National Park in 1929 and Fiordland National Park in 1952.

Three factors led to the location of most of the reserve areas in the uplands. The first was the European alpine tourist tradition, the second was the impossibility of milling the timber and developing the land in an economic way, and the third was probably the long reign of a Liberal Government. From 1891 to 1912, over what should be regarded as the formative years of conservation development in New Zealand, one main aim of Liberal planning was to 'put the small man on the land'. In the jargon of the times, they set out to bust the big estates, which already encompassed much of the open tussock grassland areas. That was the rhetoric, but the reality was that the estates sailed on relatively unscathed and much of the land opened up for development came from the Crown and Maori owners. Fortunately for the developing tourist industry, scenically valued landscapes often coincided with areas unsuited for settlement, but wherever lands contained both scenic and settlement value, the settlers moved in and scenic values were lost.

Where local sentiment ran high enough to raise money for purchase of land on the now-burgeoning urban fringe, like Kennedy's Bush on Christchurch's Summit Road, the reserves were usually small. Scenic reserves were very rarely designated at the same time as lands were opened to agriculture, and where it occurred, the reserves were small and of irregular shapes, which pushed up the cost of fencing and viable management.

Similarly, the scenic corridor reserves created along major tourist routes like the North Island's Main Trunk Railway were of inappropriate shape, both for fencing and management and also for biological viability. A significant pattern had been set and accepted by Government in the early 1900s. The modern scientifically based conservation movement, which aims to secure ecologically representative sites covering the full diversity of vegetation types, has been struggling against this institutionalised pattern ever since.

Perhaps it was the knowledge of the fate of the moa, or the fact that as the conservation movement began to slip into gear, the native dawn-, day- and evening-bird choruses were being replaced by those of the acclimatised exotic birds, that attention was first focused on the birds. As the vast bulk of New Zealand's songbirds were forest-dwelling, the native grasslands and other more open plant communities tended to be left out of the reserve list. Seventy per cent of the reserves in Canterbury were beech and podocarp forest, which, in pre-European times, had covered only eleven per cent of the area. Short tussock grassland, which in 1850 covered half of the local landscape, was represented in only four per cent of the reserves.

The Gifford Party sets out to explore the Milford Track area, 1890.
ALEXANDER TURNBULL LIBRARY

Securing a fully representative series of reserves that would give protection to all unique endemic plants and animals of Moa's Ark was, and still is, an uphill battle. Even the lowland forest reserves have come into contention, for they are, at least in the eyes of certain types of forester, 'vast areas of profitable resource, going to waste, sterilised by the greenies'.

It had to be the voluntary conservation groups who took up the challenge of swaying public, and hence government, opinion towards the true economics of scientifically based conservation. In recent times it was an economic proposition — to smelt aluminium at Bluff and to raise the level of Lake Manapouri — which enraged the general population of New Zealand and led to the signing of a petition against the proposal by 300,000 people from all over the country. The government of the day was forced to listen to the voters, and Manapouri was safe — for a while. The environmental era had begun in earnest, part of a world-wide trend of concern by long-sighted people who could see resource disasters ahead if short-sighted governments (who couldn't see beyond the next election) didn't act in the best long-term interests of the nation.

Elsewhere in the world, concern for the environment has been politicised to the point where Green politicians stand successfully against the conventional politicians on a platform of environmental concern. It is a reflection of how far general environmental standards have plunged in the last fifty years that so many voters support Green policies. Just across the Tasman Sea, as I write these words, Bob Browne and his Green Independents hold the balance of power in Tasmania, and environmental issues are front-page news in every state of Australia. But, in southern New South Wales, people are being jailed for merely being in forests and on forest roads, where they are potentially preventing foresters from logging trees. Over here in New Zealand, the scene is dramatically different — Tasman Forestry, the Department of Conservation and independent conservation organisations have concluded an agreement to stop logging in all native forests owned by Tasman. New Zealand is getting it right — and the strength of the conservation movement is what is keeping New Zealand on track. (Also, the Government is conscious that if it allows the landscape to be destroyed, then it is dissipating the resource that tourists come from all over the world to see — and that is income New Zealand sorely needs.)

Who are these powerful conservation organisations and what do they do?

The oldest-established organisation is the Royal Forest and Bird Protection Society, founded in 1923. With headquarters in Wellington, the society boasts 56,000 members, organised into strong regional groups. Its aims are to protect New Zealand's native species, natural ecosystems and landscapes, and promote an appreciation of these. The society publishes its own quarterly magazine, operates eight lodges and houses, and also owns and manages several large reserves.

The Native Forests Action Council, recently renamed the Maruia Society, has taken campaigning and well-conceived direct action from success to success. The visionaries behind this movement operate from a base in Nelson and first came to notice by leading a successful campaign against a massive and ill-conceived pulp mill based on North Westland's beech forests. The forest campaigns soon spread throughout New Zealand and gave rise in 1976 to the 341,160-signature petition, the

A green gecko, *Naultinus grayi*, on an Australian invader, *Hakea* species.

Lake Manapouri from Frazers Beach.

Maruia Declaration. This became the greenprint for subsequent forest conservation successes in key places such as Pureora, Whirinaki, Okarito and North Westland, and also, in association with the Royal Forest and Bird Protection Society, for the creation of the Department of Conservation.

The Native Forest Restoration Trust was founded as an incorporated society in 1980 to preserve and restore degraded native forests. The trust has planted over 30,000 native trees in Pureora, in the Cowan Wildlife Reserve and in other reserves in the Central North Island, and has been instrumental in saving forests in the Rangitoto Range and in east Pureora from destruction. In addition, the trust has raised funds to acquire the McGregor Memorial Reserve near Waipoua, together with the Puketi Mokau Reserve and McGregor Reserve Extension, in order to replant kauri forest.

It was the voice of a powerful coalition of these organisations that allowed a group of activists, led by Steve King, to keep vigil high in the branches of the massive totara trees at Pureora, thereby preventing the felling of the few remaining forest giants and bringing the attention of New Zealand and the world to the plight of the forests.

The Queen Elizabeth II National Trust is an independent organisation established by an Act of Parliament in 1977 to commemorate the Silver Jubilee of Her Majesty the Queen. Its principle task is to provide, enhance and protect open space for the enjoyment and benefit of the people of New Zealand. It operates through Open Space Covenants, legal agreements between the trust and a landowner to protect a particular area of open space for a specified time, or even forever. (The agreements are also binding on any subsequent owners of the land.) This device has opened the way to secure small areas of crucial and under-represented vegetation types for conservation. Areas of native bush that will not only help stabilise the local catchments, but also act as banks of local genetic stock, which can be used to reinstate and restock nearby degraded bush areas as they come on the commercial or the covenant market. The trust caters for all tastes, and also has large gardens in its care.

The only thing that was significantly missing in the enormous conservation effort — and it's true the whole world over — was serious and widespread attention to education about the natural environment, using the traditional structure of education in combination with the popular media in all its forms. So it was that the New Zealand Natural Heritage Foundation, a national non-profit organisation based at Massey University in Palmerston North, came into being.

The New Zealand Natural Heritage Foundation was established in 1988 to educate people about the natural heritage of New Zealand. With Television New Zealand the foundation has co-produced the television series *Moa's Ark* and the book of the series. The foundation's educational programme comprises resources from early childhood to tertiary level, with schools' resources written in English and in Maori. The first of the university courses — New Zealand's Natural Heritage — is already being taught, and, in addition, the foundation has set up a programme

The modern face of practical conservation — boardwalks at Goat Pass (*above*),
Mount Ruapehu (*centre*) and Opua (*below*).

DSIR Ecology Division scientists work with South Island robins in Breaksea Sound.
P. R. WILSON, DSIR

of educational tourism with a series of 'natural heritage' trails and with tourism certification, which is proving a winner. Not bad for an organisation that was only an idea at the beginning of 1987, and not launched until early 1988!

There are many other organisations at work in all the conservation fields. The World-Wide Fund for Nature, Friends of the Earth and Greenpeace all have New Zealand chapters as part of a world body of concern, campaigning and action. There are also many smaller bodies, like the Junior Naturalists, Yellow-Eyed Penguin Trust and the regional Tree Trusts, each doing vital work to save some endangered habitat or species, each an important part of the pastiche of conservation. Together with the scientific and management skills of the Department of Scientific and Industrial Research (DSIR) and the Department of Conservation (DOC), they are beginning the awesome task of refitting Moa's Ark for its most perilous voyage, into the future.

A major beacon on the horizon remains the concept of World Heritage, a concept as practical as it is sweeping. The World Heritage convention, lengthily called the 'Convention for the Protection of the World Cultural and Natural Heritage', was adopted by the General Assembly of the United Nations in late 1972. The convention provides a framework for international co-operation in conserving the world's outstanding natural and cultural properties. The designation of an area as a World Heritage site ensures that the area becomes the focus of world attention, part of the common heritage of the world's peoples.

The World Heritage site programme is administered by UNESCO, and New Zealand in 1987 had two sites, Fiordland National Park and Mount Cook/Westland National Park. The gap between the southern boundary of Westland National Park and the northern boundary of Fiordland National Park, one of the last contiguous tracts of kahikatea forest on the West Coast, was state-owned forest, with a logging moratorium. The pressures to log these forests from West Coasters desperate for jobs was very strong, and the conservation movement mounted a campaign to include the gap between the two World Heritage sites as part of an integrated South-West New Zealand World Heritage Site.

The South Westland Forest campaign reached its height in January 1989, and in February the New Zealand Government announced that it was nominating the whole of South Westland for World Heritage site status. The local residents remain unconvinced, but a major factor in the Government's strategy is the acknowledgement that logging these forests is totally uneconomic, and that the future must lie in tourism.

Throughout this long period of increasing concern and positive action, one problem has not only remained but has grown out of all proportion. The conservation ethic may be spreading, along with reserves, national parks and World Heritage sites to all corners of New Zealand, but the raiders are there already, wreaking their own special form of desecration.

Cascade Spit, South-West New Zealand World Heritage site.
NEVILLE PEAT

The Reserves and Domains Act of 1953 stated, with regard to scenic reserves, that: 'The native flora and fauna in the reserves shall as far as possible be preserved and the introduced flora and fauna shall as far as possible be exterminated.'

Easily said, almost impossible to accomplish. So much so that only twenty-four years later new legislation was drawn up in the form of the Reserves Act 1977, which states that scenic reserves are 'for the purposes of providing, in appropriate circumstances, suitable areas which by development and the introduction of flora, whether indigenous or exotic, will become of such scenic interest or beauty that their development, protection and preservation are desirable in the public interest'.

So the standing of exotic species has changed radically. They have been given a *de jure* place in the scenic reserves that form a sizeable portion of the system of protected natural areas in New Zealand.

One advantage of this legislation is the possibility of now preserving the distinctive qualities of the cultural landscape, but such acceptance could nurture a snake in the grass in an island system that is still devoid of serpents.

Another problem is lodged deep in the psyche of New Zealanders, and dates from the days of early settlement. A good example of a scenic reserve is Riccarton Bush, that 7.5-hectare reserve now surrounded by suburban Christchurch. A remnant of the kahikatea swamp forest association, the area has been protected privately since the 1850s. At that time a ring of oak trees was planted around the bush in an effort to provide shelter from the wind. As early as 1882 it was realised that this solution was not entirely satisfactory, as the oak trees were tending to inhibit the adjacent indigenous flora. Over a hundred years after the trees were planted, the Trustees of Riccarton Bush decided in 1974 that the reserve would benefit from removal of the oaks, and in 1981, with New Zealand Forest Service assistance, trial fellings began. Almost immediately some members of the public protested about the removal of the century-old oaks. The opposition to felling the trees was a spontaneous and emotive response, which overlooked their adverse influence on the indigenous species and the fact that a considerable area of oaks in a more appropriate parkland setting exists in the adjacent grounds of Riccarton House.

In this case the decision-making process was very slow, but unearthed a real problem in altering the perception that oaks are necessarily beautiful wherever they grow, and of convincing some people that the New Zealand bush is equally beautiful and worth preserving. All over the country the mind-set passed down from the early settlers — that anything native should be replaced by something imported from England — is part of a gung-ho, 'if it grows, cut it down', chainsaw mentality, which was appropriate for the settlers not so long ago but is totally out of place with modern times.

The argument goes on. Meanwhile, the hand-to-hand fighting to save the most endangered of all the native passengers of Moa's Ark continues apace in the lifeboats.

To the Lifeboats!

In 1892, when the Earl of Onslow, Governor of New Zealand, asked an assembly of Maori chiefs for a name for his newly born son, they asked him to call the boy Huia, the name of their most sacred bird. One of the chiefs said, 'There yonder is the snow-clad Ruahine Range, the home of our favourite bird. We ask you, oh Governor, to restrain the Pakeha from shooting huia, that when your boy grows up he may see the beautiful bird which bears his name.'

Sadly, only thirty years later, the huia was recorded as extinct, shot out of existence for trophy and for its feathers. Its song is a memory, its beauty still on show, gathering dust in museums and private collections across the world. However, it was this Maori plea that led to the designation of the first island reserves. The Earl of Onslow was not only a great Governor but also an ardent conservationist and lover of nature, and it was through his influence that, in 1892, the Government issued an edict that no huia was to be killed anywhere in New Zealand. What is more, throughout the 1890s, sanctuary islands began to be established. Resolution Island in Dusky Sound, Little Barrier Island in the Hauraki Gulf, Kapiti Island near Wellington, and Motuara in the Marlborough Sounds. These sanctuaries are still of crucial importance today.

The fact that island sanctuaries were being set aside as lifeboats, the only hope for the continued survival of a long list of the passengers of Moa's Ark, indicates the sad state of affairs on board the mother ship, even in the waning years of the last century. Not just because of people with guns, axes and fires, but because of the raiders they had brought and continued to bring with them. Thanks to the increasing presence of the mammalian stormtroopers (rats, mustelids, cats), life on the mainland had become increasingly impossible for Old Beak Head and many other endemic reptiles, Hamilton's frog, giant wetas, giraffe weevils, saddlebacks, stitchbirds, kakapo, kokako, bush wren, piopio, takahe, shore plover, laughing owl and bats.

Something had to be done and quickly, if mass extinction was not to become the order of the days ahead. None of the schemes for transferring the huia to these island sanctuaries ever succeeded, thanks to bickering between government departments. However, even if some huia had been transferred they would have probably failed, because the raiders were already at home on the islands. Rats swim strongly, but stoats swim better, and when the 'rat wave' had passed through the forest and decimated the birds, the stoats came after, seeking the rats and anything else they could find.

It became obvious that if the offshore islands were going to be used as lifeboats of survival, they had to be cleared of raiders and refitted and rigged with their original vegetation to provender and protect the crew. Refitting and rerigging meant the eradication of browsers — the deer, possum, rabbits, goats, pigs and kiore, all formidable tasks in themselves. Clearing the raiders was going to be much more of a problem, for the list included rats, cats and stoats. 'Impossible,' some said. 'A waste of time and money,' said others. But nothing is impossible when it comes to the New Zealand conservation movement.

In the late 1970s it was a just-articulated dream, but in the late 1980s it is a fact. We can eradicate rats (and cats) from offshore islands, making them truly islands of hope and lifeboats of survival. The first major success was in Fiordland, where the small nine-hectare island of Hawea and its much larger neighbour Breaksea Island (170 hectares) were targeted as possible sites to release the remnants of the Fiordland kakapo population. Norway rats had arrived in Fiordland aboard the *Resolution*, Cook's second ship, which tied up to a tree in Pickersgill Harbour in Dusky Sound in May 1773. A gangplank was put ashore and the rats must have disembarked to discover an unsuspecting fauna just waiting to be eaten. There was no Customs and no quarantine, so the rats spread like a tidal wave through the forests. Kiore were already present, brought by the Maori in earlier times. Repeated re-invasion of rats would have occurred after Cook's visit as the seal-hunting ships tied up on the island in the fiords. But it was not rats that were the cause of the first failure in lifeboat conservation in New Zealand — it was stoats, acting as amphibious pirates.

Richard Henry was a pioneer conservationist who lived on Pigeon Island in Dusky Sound for fifteen years from 1894. His task was to transfer kakapo, kiwi and weka to safety on the first of the offshore lifeboats. The attempt was doomed to failure — Pigeon Island was overrun with rats, and eventually the stoats arrived. When the stoats boarded the lifeboat they cleared up the rats but ate the birds as well, and Richard Henry left Fiordland in 1908 for Kapiti Island, which is far enough offshore to be safe from stoats.

Breaksea Island and Hawea were free of stoats, but evidence of boom-and-bust rat populations was everywhere, although deer had never reached these islands. So refitting the lifeboats was simple, but clearing the raiders remained as a major task. Newer and more effective poisons were available, and in the early 1980s the New Zealand Wildlife Service, DSIR Ecology Division and the Lands and Survey Department were beginning to believe that they were making an impact on rat populations on small islands in the Hauraki Gulf and the Marlborough Sounds. The real incentive to succeed on larger islands lay in the lizard population of rat-free Wairaki Island, which is very small and only 300 swimmable metres away from Hawea. On Wairaki Island, the Fiordland endemic skink, *Leiolopisma acrinasum*, is so common that on sunny days the rocks seem to be alive with lizards. Their presence, coupled with the discovery of at least two large weevils only recently known to science, means that this tiny island represents a precious storehouse of lifeboat survivors — sufficient reason to eradicate rats on nearby islands to ensure that the fauna of Wairaki survived unscathed.

Preparation for eradicating the raiders on Hawea Island began in 1985 with a series of baseline studies, and in early 1986 poison baits were set out in plastic tubes (to prevent birds from eating them) on a forty-metre grid over the island. The baits were checked and replaced daily, and were seemingly enjoyed by the rats, who

The Fiordland skink, *Leiolopisma acrinasum*.
BRUCE THOMAS, DSIR

Rowley Taylor, of the DSIR's Ecology Division, inspects
rat damage on Breaksea Island before the eradication
programme.
BRUCE THOMAS, DSIR

Breaksea, Hawea and Wairaki Islands
— 'lifeboats' in Fiordland.
R. H. TAYLOR, DSIR

Before the possums — northern rata in flower.

After the possums — dead rata dominate the canopy.

Kaka keep watch from the verandah of the ranger's house on Kapiti Island.

sometimes waited at the tubes for a second helping. Twelve days after the start of the programme, no more baits were being taken. Six weeks later, in late May 1986, rats were officially declared eradicated from Hawea Island.

Rats have also been removed from Breaksea, Whale and Korapuki Islands, feral cats have been eradicated from Little Barrier and Cuvier Islands, and, most significant of all, the possum population of Kapiti and Codfish Islands has been extinguished. Goats have also been cleared from many of these islands. The effort involved in killing the last possum on Kapiti is an epic story itself, particularly because the steep, forested, westerly face of the island plunges almost vertically into the sea from about 300 metres at the high point. Persistence paid off, and as the lights of the Kapiti possums went out, one by one, up came the play and the players of the native flora, released from browsing bondage by the dedication of a small group of committed conservationists and skilled trappers. Another lifeboat of hope is afloat for the future.

Tiritiri Matangi

The camera crew of the *Moa's Ark* film project and myself are among the lucky few who have been fortunate enough to visit a number of New Zealand's island sanctuaries. We have had the immense privilege of walking back through these windows of time to hear the chorus of native birds and the buzz of native insects and to see in full flower the nectar-rich shrubs on which they feed. It is a truly wonderful experience, even if certain elements of the endemic fauna sometimes get in the way, especially when you are not actually filming them. While trying to demonstrate the depth of the litter layer on possum-free Kapiti, it was impossible to see the forest floor for a family of wekas, who appeared to be auditioning for a spot in a Disney wildlife adventure. Even when they kept out of camera-shot, the noise they made arguing with weka in the next-door territory made continuity a nightmare.

Although the whole conservation movement is working flat out to free the life-boats from raiders and prepare them to receive their precious castaways, it is fully aware of the problems of the élitist facet of sanctuary life. If it is only the experts, the camera crews, conservationists and the like who can have the pleasure of seeing the wildlife at first hand, why should the rest of New Zealand bother to support them? Why should the general public continue to support the work of conservation, both by voice and subscriptions, let alone taxes and votes? It is a Catch-22 situation — if the public cannot directly benefit from access to sanctuaries, their support may dry up; but too many people darting about all over the place can love a sanctuary to death.

As the conservation fraternity gazed out to sea from the shores of urban Auckland, the idea of an 'open sanctuary' came up with the sun. Why not provide an island sanctuary that would welcome people and where people would have an input? Tiritiri Matangi is the first of these sanctuaries.

Tiritiri Matangi was probably originally inhabited by members of the Kawerau tribe. They built the pa, called Tiritiri Matangi, from which the island gets its name. Their main settlements developed on the western side of the island wherever there was good access to the sea, for they were accomplished at fishing the choppy waters of the Hauraki Gulf.

Archaeological remains include terraces for whare, cooking sheds and pits for kumara storage. Below the terraces and along the beach are middens from which lots of different types of shells and the bones of fish, birds, dogs and kiore have been found. It would appear that every ridge between Pa Point and Wattle Creek has been modified in some way, and there is good evidence of a thriving settlement on the coast of North-East Bay as well.

In 1821, Ngapuhi war parties, armed with muskets, swept south from their home in the Bay of Islands and forced the local Maori to flee to their relatives on the mainland around Waikato. Returning some twenty-six years later, they were soon faced by a new invasion, this time by European settlers. From 1854 onwards, sheep were grazed on the island, and despite appeals to the Maori Land Court, the title to the land was finally vested with the Crown.

Full farm management was placed in the hands of Joseph Schollum in 1894, and pigs, rabbits, goats, quail, pheasants and sheep enjoyed the grazings on a large part of the island. Francis Dennis took over the lease two years later; a remittance man himself, he unremittingly burned off and cleared what forest was left, although the native Christmas tree was protected under the terms of the lease. The island was sown down in white clover and cocksfoot, and the rabbit population thrived despite repeated attempts at eradication. In 1901 the Hobbs family took possession of the potential and the problems, and this family connection lasted for seventy years, during which the rabbits were eradicated and sheep and cows were ferried to the mainland in the good scow *Vesper* to be sold.

The Hauraki Gulf Maritime Park Board took over responsibility for the island in 1971, and by the end of that year it was ungrazed except by kiore and the vegetation began to regenerate. From the tiny patches of modified vegetation that remained, it was obvious that the original native bushland would have been dominated by pohutukawa, with kohekohe and taraire especially in the sheltered valleys. After a few years it became clear that natural regeneration was going to be a very slow business, for the obvious reasons of lack of seed material, problems of germination in the stock-compacted soil and competition with the aggressive alien grasses. To speed the process it was decided to begin a programme of tree planting, with the help of local conservationists and schoolchildren ferried out from the mainland.

The dream of Tiritiri as an open reserve, which the public could visit at will as long as they behaved themselves, might well have foundered, for a number of conservationists thought that it would never work and the public could never be relied on. However, when the call for help went out, the enthusiasm and involvement of all those who volunteered their labour or donated money was fantastic. World-Wide Fund for Nature in New Zealand adopted Tiritiri as one of their major projects, and it was their public fund-raising drive that enabled the revegetation programme to take root.

Tree nurseries, potting, classroom and accommodation facilities were developed in the buildings that nestle around the 20.5-metre lighthouse, built in 1865. The original lamp was first lit on 21 December 1864 and was fuelled by whale oil; the tower was painted red, perhaps in shame. Its light was clearly visible from forty-five kilometres and must have guided many a whaling ship to the safety of an Auckland berth. In 1956 the installation of an eleven-million candle-power xenon lamp made it the most powerful light in the Southern Hemisphere and then, as now, the tower was painted an incandescent white.

It was this bright white light which greeted us, complete with an excited crowd of youngsters from a number of schools in Auckland, as we made our way through decidedly choppy seas for a planting session on the island. Despite a surfeit of pills and special pressure-point anti-seasickness bracelets, the journey taught us the real

The landing at Tiritiri Matangi Island.

meaning of the name Tiritiri Matangi — 'wind tossing about'. But we were soon at the pier, to be greeted by the ranger and his wife, Mr and Mrs Walter, who have made the island their home and its revegetation their lives' work. We were led up the zig-zag path to the tree nursery and open-air schoolroom. *Mal de mer* was soon forgotten as we were introduced to live kiore and told that because they were seed-eaters, they caused no direct harm to the native birds, which were now living in safety on the island. Small populations of tui, fantails, silvereyes, grey warblers and even bellbirds were present when the island was taken over as a reserve. Ground-dwellers like pukeko and spotless crakes were doing well, as were many aliens, including brown quails, hedge sparrows, starlings, mynas, yellowhammers and goldfinches; the list, the pictures and the odd alien flying by or hopping in made me feel quite at home.

We were also told how some of the much rarer birds — saddlebacks and parakeets, with the little spotted kiwi, takahe and whiteheads next — had been introduced by the old Wildlife Service and that it was hoped that some of the kowhai we were about to plant would provide sufficient flowers that the tui would stay on the island the year round. And, 'wait for it', we were told (for some of us were already making for our spades), with further planting of the right sort of trees and shrubs, the whitehead and stitchbird may, one day, feel at home.

We were off, complete with saplings, shovels and picks to do our bit to revegetate the island. It was hard work and we were glad the wind was blowing to keep us cool

The ranger of Tiritiri Matangi briefs visitors.

Spade power — revegetating in action.

213

Planting the future.

Cabbage trees, flax and regenerating forest on Tiritiri Matangi.

in the hot sun. We soon found out why the native birds don't like the open sun-scorched grassland, although the native harrier, hawking above, didn't seem to mind. We also discovered why the seedlings found the hard, compacted soil such a problem; we had to dig our way through before a handful of humus and a handful of fertiliser completed the job. There were several hundred saplings to be planted and the mix had to be got just right. A cabbage tree clump here, kowhai, pohutukawa there and, downslope, a glade of taraire and kohekohe, and don't forget the native flax and fuchsia.

Many eager hands, small as some of them were, made heavy work a little lighter and a lot of fun, and soon the job was complete. There was still a lot to see and learn as we made our way back through one of the better bits of woodland. Both parakeet and saddleback need holes in which to nest, and in the absence of old, gnarled pohutukawa trunks, complete with natural nest sites, boxes have been installed specially for the purpose. Quiet! Shh! Silently we made our way up the hill and approached the box to see if anyone was at home — and they were. A female saddle-back in all her glory appeared from the box and, unafraid, rested in full view before she flew off. The open sanctuary of Tiritiri Matangi is all about bringing rare wildlife out of dusty glass cases, full into public view. It also takes pressure off the more vulnerable sanctuaries and increases people's resolve to ensure the future survival of the living treasures of Moa's Ark.

Well, we were all convinced and, despite a very rough crossing back to the mainland, the talk was about what the party had seen and learned. 'Isn't it fantastic,' the children chorused, 'all those trees were grown from seed collected on the island. 'Local genetic stock, you know.' It was like listening to a bunch of budding David Attenboroughs. 'What would happen if the tree-climbing black rat or the brown rat got introduced by mistake, or visitors set fire to the bush? What would happen to the poor baby birds?' Lessons well learned and, I am sure, knowledge passed on to parents waiting with some trepidation at the dock (it had been a very rough crossing).

So rough that the next day the news reported the grounding of a fishing boat on Tiritiri. Horror! What about the danger of rats leaving the sinking ship and invading the open lifeboat? No need to worry, the news pictures showed the Walters inspecting the boat and laying baited traps, both within it and in the vicinity of the wreck. Traps made of long plastic tubes so that the rats but not the birds could get at the poison.

The planting of the thousands of trees needed to support the growing number of introduced and resident native birds is a huge task. Conservation groups, service organisations, sports clubs and schools are among those who are doing the work. The programme will require continuing voluntary participation and many more generous donations in the years to come. Tiritiri Matangi is an experimental project that is being continuously monitored, and the future of other potential open sanctuaries hinges on its success.

Mahoenui and Mapara

'Takahe, one of the fabled, flightless birds of New Zealand, once thought to be extinct, now on open display to the public, just off the coast of metropolitan Auckland.' Impossible! No, actual fact, thanks to the rediscovery of this elusive bird by Geoffrey Orbell, and Trojan work by conservationists, both in the field and at the Mount Bruce Research Station. *Notornis* (which holds the world record for the production of all-organic manure at nine linear metres a day) is breeding in captivity and is ready for relocation in an open sanctuary. With this and all the other stories of success, it is little wonder that thoughts are being turned towards the next step — away from the lifeboats and back to a refit of the Ark itself.

Such a radical idea was certainly nudged in the right direction by the discovery of a 300-hectare patch of gorse at Mahoenui, which is now a nature reserve. But gorse, *Ulex europaeus*, is a raider, one of the worst, a noxious plant; it must be got rid of! Not this patch, say the conservationists, including the Department of Conservation, for living within its spiny protection is a population of giant wetas, which, before this discovery, were listed as extinct on the mainland. A scientific description of the plant is explanation enough: 'A densely spiny shrub, spines 1.5–2.5 cm, rigid, deeply furrowed', ideal for the armour-plated wetas to retreat among, safe from rats and mice alike. Their own inland-island sanctuary, open to the public but closed to the most disastrous of the raiders, a gorse hedge against extinction. Knowing that most people do not like the thought, let alone the look, of wetas, and have been taught to hate gorse, DOC knew that a gorse weta sanctuary would not rate high on the popularity lists — but they took the plunge and went ahead anyway, and now the giant wetas and their gorse habitat are safe.

The Royal Forest and Bird Protection Society went further than this and published an appeal for weta boxes. In multiples of $10, the money is still coming in and helps to fund a breeding programme and scientific study of the weta. Wetas may not look very nice, but they don't bite, they don't sting, they are vegetarians doing no one any harm; and if handled with care, they can make very good friends — honest!

Not far away from Mahoenui, over the pumice hills, lies Mapara and here, perhaps enthused by the growing band of wetaphiles, DOC took the goat by the horns and made one of their most ambitious steps to date, aiming to put Mapara on the world map of conservation as an inland-island. Mapara comprises 15,000 hectares of native forest, much of which is scarred with tracks and skid lines, for it has been heavily logged over. The forest covers over-steepened, pumice-based countryside, and is set in a sea of farmland. En route to film the conservation work, we met a large mob of sheep, complete with two well-trained dogs and a farmer

Female giant weta on gorse at Mahoenui.

leading his horse; a much rarer sight today than it was when I learned geography at school. We were also met by an even greater rarity, one of the most evocative sounds on earth, the call of the kokako.

Despite the fact that Mapara is infested with goats, possums, rats, stoats, cats and a host of other introductions, all of which compete with the kokako for lifespace, this fabulous bird is not uncommon. The question must be: for how much longer? Faced with the dilemma of looking after this rare and endangered songster, relocation on some suitable offshore island has always been the *modus operandi*. Not so in the case of Mapara. DOC has decided to treat this tract of forest as an island and manage its inhabitants in such a way that the native plants and animals benefit.

The whole area is now fenced, itself a mammoth job. We crossed the river, complete with camera crew, two dogs, hunters plus guns, possum traps and bait, and a lot of combined conservation wisdom. The local DOC people are certainly fit, so I puffed along at the back. I was glad that I was last, because I am somewhat squeamish when it comes to killing things and I didn't look as possums were despatched and goats were shot. But I will never forget the sight of one of the hunters descending a steep track complete with a large goat on his back — a cross between Charles Atlas and the Devil incarnate.

We filmed the works amidst signs that this new form of management is already successful. The forest has a good stratum of undergrowth and a range of seedlings of native trees and shrubs were in evidence. However, most important of all, the song of the kokako was with us all the way. So well versed are the hunters, the researchers and the managers with their local kokako population that each bird can be recognised and is known by name. As management continues, rollcalls can be taken and the population checked in each block of the reserve.

DOC is the first to admit that it is a long-term job and couldn't be accomplished without the help of many other bodies, including the conservation groups and the local farmers. Mapara will cost money and DOC is looking for sponsors. If New Zealand can find sponsors for weta boxes, I am sure the money will come rolling in for kokako, especially as Alan Saunders and his team believe that once the restoration work is complete, the whole scheme could be managed by one full-time gamekeeper conservation manager, with help from volunteers.

DOC's plan for the future of kokako goes something like this.

In large forest tracts with a viable kokako population, like Puketi or northern Urewera, management will concentrate on land protection and advocacy, vigorous animal control and monitoring the birds and their habitats.

In medium-sized forest blocks with sufficient kokako present to raise doubt as to whether it is a viable population or not, the kokako will be intensively managed. This will involve surveying and subsequent monitoring of kokako and their habitats in conjunction with stock and wild-animal control. Apart from nest location and protection, it is in these populations of indeterminate status that research will also be carried out. Examples of such sites are Oparau, Mapara, Kaharoa and Rotoehu. Apart from kokako distribution and the feasibility of management, there is obviously a host of other ecological parameters to be considered as part of site selection, and this will require scientific and management inputs with a national perspective.

Lastly, low numbers of kokako exist in small, isolated forests and relocating these birds to larger, managed forest blocks will be considered. Leaving kokako in forest remnants will be sanctioned only if intensive management, including monitoring, is proposed, and small blocks are not the best areas for such management.

The kokako is an endangered bird that requires large and relatively intact forest areas free from the ravages of fellers, munchers and browsers if it is to survive much longer. As an indicator of the health of indigenous forest ecosystems, and of our effectiveness as ecological managers, we really could not ask for a better challenge! And what a challenge, to refit large parts of the decks of Moa's Ark so that overseas visitors can see and hear the kokako, watch the giant weta and stare at the takahe. New Zealanders can begin to stand proud on the decks of Moa's Ark if this trend continues.

Graeme Platt's Place

Our last window onto the future opens within the suburbs of metropolitan Auckland at a specialist native tree nursery. It is no ordinary garden centre, full of plastic gnomes and hybrid tea and floribunda roses. These have their place, but not in Graeme Platt's new scheme of things. To him, they and all the other exotic garden introductions are plants of a more colonial past, a past that created the quarter-acre section bounded by a well-trimmed hedge, edged with herbaceous borders which followed the line of the garden path to surround the house with flowers. All this was set in a sea of immaculate greensward, dotted with fruit and specimen trees drawn from the four corners of the earth. A hidden kitchen garden and an incinerator behind the garage completed a neat and tidy picture, which could have been taken in every English-speaking country around the world — a picture of the most energy- and nutrient-intensive ecosystem on earth.

Thanks, in no small part, to Graeme Platt and a small band of native plant devotees, the classic colonial idea of a garden is being recycled on the compost heap of new thinking, to be replaced with the much easier to maintain and manage native bush garden. The new garden order is:

Instead of the hedge, mixed bush, some growing to five metres tall, provides privacy and a windbreak. Included among the diversity on offer are kohuhu, tarata, puka, kapuka and two wonderful olearias, *O. albida* with white flowers and *O. paniculata* with its whispy, almost smoky, foliage.

Tussock grassland makes the edging tool obsolete and relegates the mower to a lesser role. Amongst the native tussocks, ground-cover plants like mountain totara, ground bush lawyer, hebes and coprosmas keep out the weeds, yet leave room for a variety of alpines, and there are a lot to choose from. A rock garden sets them off to perfection, bringing the screes of Tongariro and Nelson down to sea level, and the Southern Alps into home perspective.

Tree-fern glades provide welcome shade for the pool and barbecue, for who needs plastic umbrellas when you can have mamaku, ponga, wheki ponga and para, nature's own green-golden parasols, to do the job with elegance? What is more, they do not need storage and repair at the onset of winter. They also provide exactly the right sort of shade in which many of the smaller ferns for which New Zealand is so deservedly famous can thrive. Imagine Prince of Wales feathers and kidney fern growing frond by frond with *Psilotum* and *Tmesipteris*, two of the world's ancient forms of land plants.

Lawns there must be for space to rest and to play, space enough to be able to stand back and enjoy the spectacle of your creation and space for specimen trees. Northern rata, kowhai, totara, rimu and, of course, kauri, are all, even in their young phase, objects of immense latent majesty. Likewise, a clump of toetoe provides a creamy white centrepiece which changes with the seasons and with every breath of wind. But please avoid the look-alike immigrant, pampas grass, which is now rampaging over so much of the country.

If the plot is large enough, a swamp garden is a must, for there amongst the pukatea and swamp maire, two of New Zealand's most typical plants thrive to perfection. They are, of course, the cabbage trees and the flaxes. Graeme admits that he was once a great advocate of the variegated and red- and pink-striped cultivars of the latter. Now he prefers the natural colours, shapes and textures of the leaves and flower spikes selected by the Maori people over a thousand years of craftwork.

Leading you up the garden path, *Cotula*, *Nertera* and *Pratia* edge the stones which pave the way past the rock garden and on to the compost heap, the former overflowing with an ever-increasing collage of native colours and textures, the latter, with the help of native earthworms and creepy crawlies, making good, all-New Zealand organic compost.

For those who are asking, 'But what about colour and spectacle?' all I can say is take a walk around Platt's place, invest in the future and take some home for yourself. *Clianthus*, from white through cream to rose, golden kowhai, yellow *Brachyglottis*, unforgettable forget-me-nots from the Chatham Islands. Magenta, violet and pink through white hebes, rata red and pohutukawa, crimson for Christmas, what more could any gardener want?

The list is long and is getting longer, for Graeme spends much of his time away in the bush, hunting for new stock. Two or three trips a year take him the length and breadth of Moa's Ark, searching for seeds. His favourite haunts are the most inaccesible places on offshore islands, places where people and the raiders that came with them have not reached or been able to despoil. There, in nooks and crannies beyond the reach of thar, chamois or even goats, he searches for the survivors, the rare and unusual, the almost extinct: a slightly deeper colour, very hairy or hairless leaves, silvers, browns and reds, flowers that bloom at different seasons and blooms that stay open and perfect for a little longer, fruits, seeds and even roots that add variety to the seasons and the landscape.

Natural variety is not only the spice of evolution but of Graeme Platt's life and livelihood. He is all the time drawn on by the excitement of finding something new, something as yet overlooked by science. Perhaps his most surprising discovery to date was ratakawa or pohutarata, a hybrid between rata and pohutakawa, these two already-famous trees. Hybrids are not uncommon in nature, a cross between two related species indicating that the process of evolution is still carrying on apace. Hybrids between two tree species take a lot of looking up for, something at which Graeme has become adept, for he has discovered that the best seeds are always found on the highest branches. Climbing has become part of the Platt act and, although he can scale the forest giants with ease, he has not as yet come up with an explanation as to why the best should be at the top.

Offshore islands are treasure houses of native plants, for not only have they escaped, to a greater or lesser extent, the havoc caused by the raiders, but Platt also enthuses on the fact that their plants often have larger leaves and are more luxuriant in their growth. This even goes for specialities like the nikau palm, where the fronds from the Great Barrier Island population arch gracefully from the centre, unlike those of the mainland, which tend to grow straight up.

Variety and quality are Graeme's stock in trade, and time and again he finds the best seed source comes from those areas where native bush still reigns supreme. If he wants good, vigorous kauri, he goes to Waipoua or another large stand, where a good intermix of genetic diversity ensures a vigorous next generation, so much so that only ten per cent of the seed has to be rejected. Given the right organic and nutrient-rich conditions, the growth rate has to be seen to be believed. Go to Platt's Place and see it for yourself.

If only there were more places like Waipoua, Pureora and Whirinaki from which to collect. To make up for the genetic shortcomings of certain types of native bush which are left, and to ensure genetic diversity of his stock in hand, Graeme always collects seed from as many individual trees and plants as he can. Likewise with cuttings; and he never, but never, digs up or removes whole plants from the wild.

Back at the nursery, the process of selection and propagation goes on apace. Seeds are the product of pollination and sexual fusion, the main function of which is to maintain genetic variety, so they never breed absolutely true. In consequence, the seedbeds of both first and subsequent generations are always scanned for genetic novelty. With cuttings, the outcome is more predictable, for, being actual chips of the old genetic block, they should breed true. Yet even here sports can arise with characteristics all of their own.

Part of Graeme Platt's garden.

Flowers of *Tecomanthe speciosa.*
ROD MORRIS

The process of bulking the stock and keeping it all pure is a problem, especially when faced with an ever-growing population of native plant punters who drop in all the time, their itchy green fingers demanding something new. So it is that the process goes on — location, collection, propagation then dispersal to gardens, scattered not only the length and breadth of New Zealand, but across the world — a process that is today ensuring the survival of what were many endangered species.

The best story of success to date is that of *Tecomanthe speciosa.* In 1946 it was down to just one individual plant, the last one in the world, well browsed by goats on one tiny cliff location on the Three Kings Islands. Now, thanks to Graeme and others, thousands of individuals are gracing gardens all over the world. A shrub liana with wonderful white, long-lasting flowers, a plant with great horticultural capabilities, it could have become no more than a memory in the annals of botany. It was great to see the beds of *Tecomanthe* awaiting new owners in one corner of the nursery.

The role of Graeme Platt's place is threefold. It is helping to save the genetic diversity of the plants of New Zealand from extinction. It is providing a firm genetic base for all future reconstruction of native bush on degraded and eroded land. It is instilling an understanding and love of the plants that constitute native bush exactly where it is needed, in the hearts and gardens of urban dwellers. By the end of this sad century more than sixty per cent of all the human beings in the world will live in urban areas. We can only hope that most of them have access to a local Graeme Platt.

EPILOGUE

Unique is a word I try to use as little as possible. However, New Zealand *is* unique. It was the last Ark of the Covenant of Mainstream Evolution to be raided by people, and that didn't happen until some 1,000 years ago. It is also the only large piece of earth's real estate that never felt the tread, the teeth or the guile of ground-living mammals throughout its evolutionary history.

It was a haven of a unique bird, insect and plant life until people came on the scene. People destroyed so much and yet, as our brief voyage of discovery on board the Ark has shown, it is only people who can now save the rest from extinction. We have also seen that the will is there, and the expertise, for it is my opinion that when it comes to the theory and especially the practice of the conservation ethic, New Zealand leads the world.

New Zealand is thrice-blessed. She has a small human population and a relatively high standard of living, and is a good way towards energy self-sufficiency, clear of the problems of atomic power. In real terms, New Zealand has the strongest economy in the world, for if international trade stopped tomorrow, she could feed, clothe and care for all her people. Each of them could have a new wooden house every twelve years set in one of the most beautiful and challenging environments on earth. Self-sufficiency and sustainability in all things is well within her grasp, a boast few other nations could ever hope to make. Think about it!

Of course world trade isn't going to stop, but New Zealand, like all families, is faced with the scourge of the twentieth century: cash flow. How does she continue to pay her way and how does she pay for the bill to repair Moa's Ark and keep it afloat and on course into the future?

Well, just as the marine reserves off the Poor Knights point to richer days ahead for both the fish and the fishermen, so too do all the other reserves, national parks and World Heritage sites.

From the outside looking in, New Zealand is a precious green jewel floating in the enormity of the Pacific Ocean. It is a prime tourist destination, uniquely endowed to offer much more than the conventional sun, sand, golf, disco and casino holiday. It is also within easy reach of her neighbours at the other more crowded end of the Pacific rim — Japan and the United States. What is more, in modern travel terms, Europe is not all that far away. Why, it takes only eleven hours for my postcards to get to Britain, thanks to the international date line.

The tourists of tomorrow are increasingly demanding a new experience, a Grand Tour complete with an educational component that will enrich their lives in an unforgettable way. New Zealand can unashamedly cash in on the fact and it is already happening. In 1987 the mere 0.02 per cent of the world's tourists who visited New Zealand earned the country half as much income as all its agricultural exports. Double the number and think of all the ways the tourists' dollars and yens could help not only 'balance the payments' but help fund the vital work of conservation and land-care management. This work will itself have massive positive spin-offs on

223

agriculture, healing the land and the landscapes that have been ruined by profligate misuse in the past. What is more, the new organic movement could proudly produce the most pure food in the world.

There is no time or place to cry over what has been lost during the main phases of colonisation by one mammal, or by the depredations caused by the others they brought with them. Now is the time to highlight a spectacular past through their remains displayed and interpreted in museums, caves, swamps, botanical gardens

A song of survival — South Island saddleback, *Philesturnus carunculatus*.
ROD MORRIS

and wilderness areas. Despite the fact that so much of the vegetation has been lost, New Zealand still boasts all sorts of wonders of the natural world, many of which are of World Heritage status. It is my opinion that you should boast a lot more about what you have and tell the world exactly what lies in store for their visit.

New Zealand has the volcanoes and hot spots to tell the story of how the planet was created; the glaciers, the broad-braided rivers, lakes and caves to show the power of water; the cleanest of seas, well stocked with living fossils; the forests of Gondwana that were home to the moa and before that to their ancestors, the dinosaurs, and contain the biggest trees by volume, the largest fern and the largest species of moss; the rarest parrot and penguin, all world records. I was going to mention the rarest bird in the world, but, thanks to the work of New Zealand conservationists, the black robin no longer holds that distinction.

The people of the world and the people who make and will make their livelihoods from tourism on Moa's Ark have much to thank the voluntary conservation bodies for — Royal Forest and Bird, Maruia Society, QEII National Trust, Native Forest Restoration Trust and all the others have all worked tirelessly over many years to keep the green base of the tourist resource safe from despoliation. And an on-going vote of thanks must go to the officers of the new Department of Conservation, whose Trojan work is not only managing the resource but is now redeveloping key parts for the future. Thanks are also due to the New Zealand Natural Heritage Foundation, working hard to produce the educational experience which will help young New Zealanders to grow up appreciating the value of their still wonderful natural heritage.

For all this, these eminently marketable features, the true 'futures' of world investment, are wrapped up in a landscape that includes some of the most beautiful and dramatic on earth: North Cape, the Bay of Islands, Coromandel, Tongariro National Park, Castle Hill, the Southern Alps, South Westland, Milford Sound . . . I could go on and on.

This is the greenest country in the world in more ways than one, shouting a message of hope to a dying world. I tell you, if New Zealand can't make it work, the rest of the world hasn't got a chance.

LONG LIVE MOA'S ARK AND ALL THAT SAIL ON HER.

6 February 1990

Dear Uncle Nem,

Sorry I took so long to reply to your postcard.
Thanks for the stamp and the experience.

David Bellamy

P.S. Wish you were here.

INDEX

Aciphylla horrida, *112*

Alpine plants, colonisation by, 111–5, 117, 119

Amphibians, 49, 54

Anderson, Atholl, 135, *136*

Andreaea rupestris, 40

Antarctic Convergence, 93–4, 97, 100

Aupouri Tombolo, 146–51

Aoraki. *See* Mount Cook

Bacteria, 26

Baleen whales, 100

Barnacles, 111

Bellbirds, 87–8

Bird conservation, 197, 212, 215

Birds, extinct, 145

Black button daisy, 111

Black coral (*Antipathes aperta*), 30, *30*

Blackberry (*Rubus fruticosus*), 169

Boardwalks, *200*

Brachiopods, 29

Bracket fungus, *129*

Breaksea Island, 206, *207*

Bridge to Nowhere, 164, *165*

Bull kelp (*Durvillea antarctica*), 106, *153, 154*

Bush wren (*Xenicus longipes*), 87, 145

Buttercups, *110*, 111, 115

Cabbage tree (*Cordyline australis*), *104*

Canadian pondweed (*Elodea canadensis*), 170–1

Candytuft (*Iberis amara*), 173

Canterbury Plains, *132–3*, 139

Cape Foulwind, 106–8

Cape Reinga, *192–3*

Cascade Spit, *203*

Castle Hill, *114*, 115

Castle Hill buttercup, *114*, 115

Cat, feral, 171, 209

Cat's eye snail, 46

Cetaceans, 97–8

Chemical pest control, 166

Chew Chong, 162–3

Chlorophyll, 24

Cladia, 46

Coal, 49

Conifers, 59, 75

Conservation movement, 195–204

Cook, James, 158, 160

Cook, William Douglas, 187, 188

Coppicing, 190–1

Cord grass (*Spartina*), *178*, 179

Cortaderia fulvida, *104*

Cyanobacteria, 24, *25*

Cyathea dealbata, *51*

Cyclone Bola, 185, 188; damage by, *186*

Daisies, 115

Dawsonia superba, 36–9, *37*

Deer (*Cervus*), 169–70

Deer exclosures, 81

Department of Conservation, 201, 202, 216, 218

Dicroidium, 58

Dinosaurs, 64, 71, 72, 73, 75

Divaricating shrubs, 167, *168*

Doak, Wade, 32, 33

Dobbins, Alex, 90, *90*

Double Bay, Otago Peninsula, *95*

Douglas, Charlie, 195

Dragonflies, 50

Drilling rig, *51*

Dune systems, 148–9; forested, 76

Durham Cathedral, 66

Eastwoodhill Arboretum, 185–8, *189*

Ellis, Leon MacIntosh, 180, 182

Ephemeropsis trentepohlioides, 40

Erosion, 76–7

European impact on land and resources, 158–66

Exotic plants and animals: introduction of, 159, 167–79, 181–4, 187–91; status of, 204

Ferns, 49–50, *51*, 75

Fertilisers, 164–5

Fiordland skink (*Leiolopisma acrinasum*), 206, *207*

Fiordland water, 27–9, 31

Fish communities, 33

Fishing net, plastic, *101*, 102

Flax resources, use of, 161

Flowering plants, 73

Forest destruction, 161–4, 180

Forest regeneration, 63–4, 139, 148, 184; on Tiri, 211–5

Fossil forest, Curio Bay, Southland, *16–8*

Fossil fuels, 50, 91, 188

Fossils, Cambrian, 32

Franz Josef Glacier, 121–5, *123*

Fur seal, 152, *154*, 159–60

Gahnia, *124*, 126, 130

Giant giraffe beetle (*Lasiorhynchus barbicornis*), 88–90

Giant salp, 35, *35*

Giant weta (*Deinacrida*), 68, *69*, 70, 88; at Mahoenui, 216, *217*

Ginger, wild, *178*, 179

Glaciations, 91, 121, 125. *See also* Ice ages

Glossopteris, 52–4; fossil leaf of, *53*

Glow-worms, 143

Goatfish (red mullet) (*Upeneichthys porosus*), *34*

Goats, 171, *171*, 209, 217

Golfball fungus (*Cyttaria gunnii*), 78, *78*

Gondwana, 29, 53, 54, 97

Gorse (*Ulex europaeus*), 177, 216

Grasses, colonisation by, 104

Great mountain buttercup, *114*, 115

Green gecko (*Naultinus grayi*), *199*

Green politics, 198

Greenhouse gases, 23, 118

Greywacke, 109

Grumman Goose, *41*

Haast buttercup. *See* Mount Baldy buttercup

Haast River mouth area, 76–7

Hamilton's frog (*Leiopelma hamiltoni*), 68, *68*

Hauraki Gulf Maritime Park Board, 211

Hauturu. *See* Little Barrier Island

Hawea Island, 206–8, *207*

Heather (*Calluna vulgaris*), 173

Hector's dolphin (*Cephalorhynchus hectori*), *101*, 102

Henry, Richard, 206

Hoiho. *See* Yellow-eyed penguin

Hokianga (kauri tree), 64, *65*

Hooker's sea lion, 152

Horticulture, Maori, 149–50, 159

Huia, 87, 205

Hymenanthera alpina, *168*

Ice ages, 116–8, 120, 149. *See also* Glaciations

Ignimbrites, 19

Invertebrates, 32

Island sanctuaries, 205–15

Jet, 158

Jew's ear fungus, 162–3, *163*

Kahikatea (*Dacrycarpus dacrydioides*), 158, *160*, 163; seed and fleshy axil of, *74*

Kaikomako (*Pennantia corymbosa*), *168*

Kaingaroa Forest, 182

Kairaru, 63

Kaka (*Nestor meridionalis*), 90, *209*

Kapiti Island, 205, 206, 209, 210

Karst landscapes, 140

Kauri (*Agathis australis*), 59–65, 158, 184; bark, *61*; bowl, *61*; cones, *61*; rikkers, *60*

Kea (*Nestor notabilis*), 118–9, *119*

Kidney ferns, 44, *44*

Kiekie, 126, 130

King, Philip Gidley, 159

King devil hawkweed, 173

Kiore, 143, 176, 212

Kiwi, 65

Kokako (*Callaeas cinerea*), *86*, 87, 217–8

Koru, 50

Krill (*Euphausia superba*), 100–2

Kumara, 149, 150

Lagarosiphon, 170–1

Lake Manapouri, 198, *199*

Lake Rotomahana cliffs, *22*

Lambswool moss, 40

Lamp shells, 29

Laughing owl (*Sceloglaux albifacies*), 145

Lichens, 46, *46*, 78

Little Barrier Island, *82–3*, 87–90, 205

Little blue penguin, 106
Liverworts, 36–40, 78
Lockwood house, 183, *183*
Loxsoma cunninghamii, 66

Mahoenui, 216
Mamaku tree ferns (*Cyathea medullaris*),
   48, 49, 51
Mammals, 75, 103
Manuka (*Leptospermum scoparium*), *151*
Maori impact on land and resources,
   138–9, 148–50, 158–9
Mapara, 216–8
Maori worm (*Megascolicidae*), 57–8, *58*
Marine organisms, colonisation by, 103
Marram grass (*Ammophila arenaria*), 169
Maruia Society, 198–201
Massey University coppice project, 188–90
Matai (*Prumnopitys taxifolia*), male cones
   of, *74*
Menegazzia, 78
Methane, 24
Middens, 148–9, *148*
Mildenhall, Professor, 53
Milford Sound, 27, *28*
Milford Track, 27, 195, *197*
Moa, 135–8, 141, 144; bones of, *136, 144*
Moeraki Bluff, 136
Monoclea forsteri, 39, *39*
Monocotyledons, colonisation by, 104, 106
Mosasaur skull, *72*
Mosquito Hill, Haast River area, *77*
Mosses, 36–40, 50, 78
Motuara, 205
Mount Baldy, 109–11
Mount Baldy buttercup, *110*, 111
Mount Bruce Research Station, 216
Mount Cook, 116–20, *117*
Mount Cook lily. *See* Great mountain
   buttercup
Mount Kaukau, 167
Mount Tarawera, *22*
Mount Tasman, *117*
Mountain beech, *80*
Mountain daisy (*Celmisia verbascifolia*), *112*
Mountain willowherb (*Epilobium crassum*),
   112
Mustelids, 174, *175*
Muttonbird, 155–7, *156*

National parks, creation of, 195, 197
Native Forest Restoration Trust, 201
Native plant nurseries, 219–22
Needle blight fungus, 182
New Zealand Natural Heritage Foundation,
   201–2
New Zealand thrush. *See* Piopio
Ngauruhoe, *37*, 109–11
Nikau (*Rhopalostylis sapida*), 106, *107*
Ninety Mile Beach, 146, 149
Nodding thistle, 174
North Auckland worm, 58
Nothofagus. *See* Southern beech
Notornis. *See* Takahe

Old man's beard (*Clematis vitalba*), 169,
   170
Onchidella, 46
Onslow, Earl of, 205
Oparara Caves, 140–5, *141, 142*
Open Space Covenants, 201
Oringi meatworks, 190
Orongorongo Forest, 167
Ourisia macrophylla, *112*

Pakihi, 122, *124*
Pancake Rocks, Punakaiki, 104–6, *105*
Parengarenga Harbour, 146, *147*
Peat, 49, 76
Penguins, 94–6, 97, 152–5
Penwiper plant, 111
Peripatus, 56–7, *57*, 167
Photosynthesis, 24–6, 32
Pigeon Island, 206
Pink and White Terraces, 20
Pinus radiata, *181*, 181–4
Piopio (NZ thrush), 87, 88
Plankton, 100
Platt, Graeme, 219–22
Podocarps, 72, 73–5
Pohutukawa (*Metrosideros excelsa*): on
   Rangitoto, 42–4, *43, 44*; on Little
   Barrier, *89*
Polynesian migrants, early, 138–9
Poor Knights Marine Reserve, 32–5
Possum, 167, 174–6, *175*, 209; damage by,
   208
Predators, introduced, 88, 96, 167–79; on
   islands, 205–9, 215

Primrose Terraces, 20
Prions, diving, 157
Prokaryotes, 23–6
Psilotum nudum, 45, *45*
Puka, 42
Pukeko, 93
Pureora Forest, 126–30, *129, 131*, 201

Quaking grass, 176
Queen Elizabeth II National Trust, 201
Quintin McKinnon, 81

Rabbit (*Oryctolagus cuniculus*), 174
Rangitoto, 41–6, *42*
Ranunculus. See Mount Baldy buttercup,
    Great mountain buttercup
Raoulia, 119
Rata, 126, *127, 208*
Rats, *175*, 176, 205–9
Recolonisation after volcanic eruption,
    42–6, 130
Red-billed gulls (*Larus scopulinus*), *47*
Reef corals, 54
Reptiles, 54
Reserves, creation of, 195–204; on islands,
    205–15
Resolution Island, 205
Rewarewa (*Knightia excelsa*), 75; flowers,
    74
Rhacomitrium field, *38*
Riccarton Bush, 92, *92*, 204
Rifleman (*Acanthisitta chloris*), *86*, 87, 88
Rimu (*Dacrydium cupressinum*), 126–8, *127*
Rock wren, 87, 119–20
Rotorua caldera, 19–20
Royal albatross (*Diomedea epomophora*),
    98–100, *99, 102*
Royal Forest and Bird Protection Society,
    198, 201, 216
Ruahine Mountains, 111
Ruapehu, *37*, 109
Rushes (*Juncus*), 173
Russell lupin (*Lupinus polyphyllus*), *172*,
    173

Saddleback, 87, 215, *224*
Sarcophyllum bollonsi, 29
Scenic and scenic corridor reserves, 195,
    197, 204

Schistochila, 40
Scree, 111
Sea foam, 108, *108*
Sea pens, 29
Sea squirts, 35
Sealing, 159–60
Seed ferns, 52–4, 75
Seed sources, 221
Shag Point excavation, 135–8
Short-tailed bat, 85, *86*, 87–8
Silver beech, Cascade River, *79*
Silver fern, *51*
Sims, Ralph, 188–90
Sinter, 20
Snake star (*Astrobrachion constrictum*),
    30–1
Snares, 152–7
Snares Island crested penguin, 152–5, *154*
Soil formation, 121–5
Sooty shearwaters. *See* Muttonbirds
South Island robins, Breaksea Sound, *202*
South Westland World Heritage site, 203
Southern beech, 77–81, *79, 80*
Spaniards. *See* Speargrasses
Speargrasses, *112*
Spelungula, 143
Sperm whales, 100–2
Sponge garden, Poor Knights, 35
Sponges, 106–8
Stellaria roughii, 112
Stephens Island, 67–70, *67*
Stephens Island wren, 67, 87
Sticta, 78
Stoats, 174, *175*, 205–6
Stony coral, 35
Stromatolites, 28
Surville Cliffs, 146, *147*, 150
Sweet briar, 176, *177*

Taiaroa Head, Otago Harbour, 98–100
Takahe, 216
Takitimu Mountains, 53
Tane Mahuta, *62, 63*, 184
Taranaki (Mt), 47–50
Tarndale Slip, 185–7
Taro, 149–50
Taupo eruption, 128–30
Taurepo (*Rhabdothamnus solandri*) flowers,
    86

Te Anau, 81
Tecomanthe speciosa, 146, 222, *222*
Tetradontium brownianum, 40
Three Kings Islands, 146
Thymus vulgaris, 176, *177*
Timber resources, use of, 161–2, 180–4
Tiritiri Matangi, 210–5, *212, 213, 214*
Toetoe, *104*
Tongariro, 36, *37*, 39
Totara (*Podocarpus totara*), *74*
Tourist industry, 195–7, 223–5
Travis Swamp, 93, *93*
Tuatara (*Sphenodon*), 68, *69*, 70

Vegetable sheep, 119, *120*
Venus's necklace, 46
Volcanic activity, 19–20, 26

Wagener Museum, Houhora, 151
Waiho River valley, 121–5
Waimangu Stream, *25*
Waipapa Ecological Area, *131*
Waipoua, 65
Wairaki Island, 206, *207*
Waitangi Treaty House and Meeting
    House, *161*

Waiuku Junior School children, *65*
Walter, Mr, 212, *213*, 215
Wandering jew (*Tradescantia virginiana*),
    177
Warbrick Terrace, Waimangu Valley, *21*
Wasp, German (*Vespula germanica*), 177,
    179
Weka, 210
Wellington Botanic Gardens, 55–8, *56*
Westland black petrel, 106
Whakarewarewa, 19
Whaling, 160
Whirinaki, 71, 75
White Terrace, 20, *21*
Wiffen, Joan, 71
Willowherbs, 111, *112*, 113
Wilson, Dr Edward, 52–3
Wood wasp, 182
World Heritage sites, 27, 66, 140, 202–3
World-Wide Fund for Nature in NZ, 211
Worms, 57–8

Yellow-eyed penguin (*Megadyptes
    antipodes*), 94–6, *95*
Yorkshire fog, 179